Digital Declutter:

The BIG Checklist to Obtain Digital Minimalism

by
D. M. Elliot

Copyright (C) 2020 D. M. Elliot
All rights reserved. No part of this book may be reproduced or used in any manner without written permission of the copyright owner except for the use of quotations in a book review.

Paperback ISBN 978-1-7355310-1-4
ebook ISBN 978-1-7355310-0-7

www.digitaldeclutterCEO.com

For you,
the overwhelmed,
the digitally disorganized,
step by step, this is for you.

Table of Contents

INTRODUCTION

1 - Your Current Digital Mess

2 - Oh, No! What Happened?

3 - Charting your Digital Life

4 - Starting Line Stats

5 - Those Are Some Overwhelming Numbers!

6 - Three BIG Steps to Jump-start Your Decluttering Process

7 - Know Your Computer: System Preferences

8 - Digital Storage Units: Right-Size Your Options

9 - Accountability Team

10 - Emails & Good Habits

11 - Habits for the Long Term

12 - Password Management

13 - Emergency!

14 - Health: Body & Soul

15 - Home, Pets, and the Internet of Things

16 - Photos

17 - Easing the Pain of Culling

18 - Cloud Files

19 - Perseverance: The Long-term Project

20 - Smartphone

21 - Website

22 - Social Media

23 - Your Digital Money Life

24 - Audio

25 - Movies & Video

26 - Reading

27 - Note-taking Apps

28 - Professional Software

29 - Travel: Business & Personal

30 - Food

31 - Education

32 - Auto

33 - Periodic Decluttering Maintenance

34 - Congratulations, You've Taken Command of Your Digital Life!

Appendix I and II

Thank You!

Acknowledgments

Notes

About the Author

INTRODUCTION

Digital Decluttering: The BIG Checklist is a big list of prompts to help you sweep out electronic cobwebs and slay those thundering herds of digital dust bunnies. It provides a systematic approach to ensure you find all the flotsam and jetsam of your digital clutter. *The BIG Checklist* is a guide with systems for you to achieve digital minimalism.

Prior to decluttering my digital life, my home was neat and organized, as was my studio space. But inside my laptop, my smartphone, and my cloud spaces, my digital life was a huge mess! It shouldn't be too complicated to organize a few files, a bunch of emails, and some photos, I thought, but I soon discovered my digital life was so much more than that.

I worked through the KonMari Method™ of tidying up and decluttering my home. I then followed that up with a day-to-day maintenance program to keep my home organized. After much searching, I was unable to find a similarly simple yet comprehensive digital declutter checklist.

The checklists and articles I found fell short in different ways. Many of the lists only helped in a few areas, and with others, the time span recommended for all of them was literally impossible to complete considering the extent of my mess. I needed a solution beyond the two-week or thirty-day lists I was finding—unless I planned on painfully tackling my clutter like an over-caffeinated university student cramming for finals.

I created *The BIG Checklist* for myself and have expanded it for your use along with tips and good habits to maintain your digital organization for the long term. *The BIG Checklist* provides clear steps that have worked for me through mapping my digital life, creating better habits, consistently completing each task, and cleaning out each digital storage space.

I feel much more relaxed when I open my devices after having decluttered my digital life.

Digital decluttering isn't about deleting everything. It's about right-sizing your digital life. If you have empty space in one room of your house, yet another area is horribly crowded, you will rearrange your home for the best flow possible. Time to do the same for your digital life.

Upon completing *The BIG Checklist*, your computer will become noticeably faster, your workflow will be noticeably smoother, and your new familiarity with your devices will make it easier to resolve problems when they arise.

Even the biggest of big checklists have limitations, and *The BIG Checklist* is no exception. *The BIG Checklist* is a big list of organized tasks and prompts. The questions are there to help you dig yourself out from under your gigantic pile of digital clutter. We each have different work, family, and lifestyle needs and wants, creating impressively different digital lives. New technologies are being created every day, so it is impossible to give specific steps for each task in every computer operating system within a single book. I have included a section of options for you to choose from when you need more information for your specific device. In addition, there is an abundance of information online that can be found through a few simple internet searches.

I've arranged the chapters of this book to systematically deal with the various areas of your lives that are encroached upon or dominated by the digital world. I have also provided you with monthly, weekly, and daily habits in which to maintain your decluttering progress for the long term. It's okay to skip around between Chapters 6 - 33 as you need to. Those without a vehicle or pets can skip whole sections of *The BIG Checklist*. However, skipping due to procrastination is only cheating yourself. You may need to persistently and repeatedly spend time in a single chapter, such as decluttering photographs from a massive backlog of vacations and birthday parties.

Organizing your digital clutter is a long-term project. I've included methods to help you track your progress, thus providing insights into improving your decluttering habits as you learn what works. Depending on the volume of your digital clutter and how much additional computer knowledge you may need to learn, it will take several months to complete.

This is a long-term decluttering adventure, a triathlon with maintenance tips to help it stick. Make the commitment to create a digitally decluttered life. Your resolution will make a huge difference towards achieving digital minimalism. By making this resolution, you promise yourself a reasonable, healthy, extended period of time in which to complete all of the tasks required to produce an uncluttered life.

So grab a friend or two and take up the challenge. A quest to sweep away digital dust bunnies is best completed with great partners at your side!

1 - Your Current Digital Mess

Frustration. Anger. Stress. Overwhelming mess. Searching for a file is like looking for that shirt you know you washed. Is it still in the dryer? Did you leave it in the pile on the sofa to be folded? Is it on the ironing board to be ironed? Wait! Did you even move that load into the dryer? Or was it simply lost between your washer and your closet?

While you are not actually tripping over your digital life like you do with laundry, it is often the same feeling. It's like a huge pile that sucks your brainpower, your time, and your money. When you do attempt to deal with it, you end up frantically searching for everything you have hiding in your computers, the cloud, SD cards, USBs, and external hard drives. In last-minute efforts, you start madly deleting photos, videos, and documents, hoping you are not deleting anything important, all so you can find space to take a few more photos or shoot just one more minute of video. Your mad decluttering under duress doesn't really help you manage your big, messy piles of digital clutter.

You are losing time to poor workflows and searching for files. You ask yourself which account you saved that project in. How much time have you lost in your life searching for lost files? You know they are in there, somewhere, hanging out in cyberspace. You know you saved it somewhere. If only you could remember where it was or if you tagged it properly. Wouldn't it be great if you had a system in place to put your files away and easily find them the next time you searched?

You receive incessant reminders from companies that your storage is running low, increasing your distractions throughout the day. Do your books send you messages that they are cluttering the living room? Of course not. Do the scattered Legos in the dining room tell you they are out of place? Not exactly, but we do know when we step on them, tripping over the various bits and stubbing our toes. Does anyone send you daily messages reminding you that your laundry needs to be folded and put away? Oh, wait, your new dryer does that!

The data storage companies know you can't see your clutter, so they need to repeatedly send you messages to clean up your data mess! Just think about those piles of photographs that are filling their storage units, along with the old tax forms you've scanned and that huge presentation you gave at work last fall. There is likely an old, abandoned blog, too. You're probably not ready for emergencies, either. In the event of a fire, hurricane, or flood, you will need your digital assets to be kept safe. On that note, you really should take photos of your possessions for the insurance company and store them in the cloud.

In addition to issues with your data, there are likely extra devices and cords scattered around your house, the car, and your work locations. You probably have piles of devices—old and new—along with all the cords, chargers, and other accessories that go with them. Plus, there are the extra cords you bought because you lost one of them, the other extra cords you bought because it was left behind when you went away on holiday, and the extra charging cords you've forgotten at home that you needed for business trips. Decluttering your hardware will help you see what you have for external storage options, with extra cords, chargers, and accessories going towards your emergency preparedness.

It can become an overwhelming headache of migraine levels to even think about tackling the mess of your digital life. Chances are that you are overwhelmingly lost on how to deal with it all. Options elude you and decision fatigue has set up house and is choosing paint colors. You need to take command of this mess systematically. A results-oriented house-cleaning system helps you take command of your physical realm. Similarly, it is time to take command of your digital realm!

Digital decluttering is more than removing excess and consolidating digital assets. It's also about right-sizing your apps, your assets, your storage, and your devices. You want to utilize all of the software's features to derive the most benefits for your time and your money.

When you are stressed out by your digital clutter, the recommendation of a digital detox is often given, meaning a full break away from your digital life with complete rest. The only problem with the usual detox methods is that when you turn the power back on again to your digital life, all the clutter is still there, most of which caused the stress in the first place. You may have tried several digital detox sessions thinking it would help, but it doesn't because you are returning to the exact same situation you left: a big black hole of data, filled with files and photos of your digital life from the past five, ten, or even twenty years! It's so much easier to be passive-aggressive about the mess and just shut your device down.

It is overwhelming to think about the amount of digital stuff that has permeated our lives. I feel that if we had control over all this stuff, a digital detox wouldn't be necessary! Therefore, it is very important for your files and accounts to be maintained. The status quo is untenable. According to a paper in Media Psychology, a digital detox from social media may not work. As reported on by The British Psychological Society website, "In one of the few experimental studies in the field, researchers have found that quitting social media for up to four weeks does nothing to improve our well-being or quality of life."

By not decluttering first, a digital detox is just an ostrich-style escape that solves nothing. When you have completed your digital decluttering prior to stepping away for a much-deserved break, you will return to an organized system instead of an entire mountain of demanding data. Using *The BIG Checklist*, a good system of habits following your big declutter, will leave you feeling as relaxed in your decluttered digital life as you do in your decluttered home, and your next digital detox will have a high chance of being successful.

On your path to minimalism, you likely took action regarding the clutter in your house. The piles of books in the corner were culled and properly shelved. Your clothes are beautifully hung, and you have space to breathe. Your kitchen is now arranged for a workflow to get everyone smoothly out the door each morning.

If you have ever read Marie Kondo's *The Life-Changing Magic of Tidying Up* and applied its principles to your clutter, your eyes have likely been opened to an amazing lightness that is relaxing and stress-free.

Keeping with these minimalist principles, you say, "No," to so many things you see in the stores. Having just spent loads of time and energy removing clutter, you don't want it building up again. You've had the elation of finding bits and pieces here and there that you really don't need and can move on to the next owner.

There has finally been enough room in your home to fully implement a house-cleaning system. What a change! Instead of taking a whole day in exasperation to finally get the house cleaning done, you can calmly take a few minutes each day, and the house actually keeps its shine, ready to have guests over within minutes.

In the same way, digital minimalism and decluttering can make your digital life much more relaxing. Being able to find those important digital assets almost immediately will greatly increase your productivity and reduce your stress.

Use *The BIG Checklist* as your guide on this journey as you mark each step and take control of your digital life.

2 - Oh, No! What Happened?

You are stressed out. The boss is demanding the project update, your youngest child is too ill to go to school today, and you've just spilled coffee onto your laptop! By the time you clean up the coffee spill, your laptop is dead. What about the data that was on it? Your mind races to remember the last time you backed up the files. You wrack your brain, hoping the project updates that your boss demands are safe. Sure, nowadays many of the programs back up automatically to the cloud, but some days there are glitches, and today is that day.

There are always stray documents or photographs that arrive on our computer and just sit. You think you'll get to them tomorrow or when things let up at work, but that day never comes. Those files, especially the ones that do automatic backups, keep piling up, and the decluttering never happens.

Any number of scenarios can happen to your devices. It could be lost in a train station. It could be stolen at the coffee shop you sometimes work from. It could get corrupted by some virus or malware. Are you prepared to deal with these scenarios?

Have you missed important deadlines due to your disorganization? Are there times when you can't find the photographs you need to complete the application or the cover image you need for your next proposal to a client? The spreadsheet you spent hours creating is lost, accidentally sent to a different cloud than you had planned— or did you accidentally save it to one of your computer drives, meaning it never left your computer, all while you've been searching for it on your USBs?

Do you have too many similar files, leaving you to wonder which file has the latest approved version of the building plans you need. Where are the citations for your engineering proposal? Has your boss come to the end of their patience with your disorganization? Are you close to losing your job due to lost data? Is a top client for your business ready to walk out? Does your clutter bleed into your accounting, leading to unpaid invoices? You're losing out on so much more than data! You're losing money!

Your old laptop has been dealing with the strain of being buried under all this clutter, which is likely the reason for your slow computer speeds. When you start thinking about all of your random files, you have reason to feel horribly overwhelmed. Your computer is drowning in clutter of every imaginable kind. It's feeling the strain of all those files as surely as you do. Lighten its load by moving files to external hard drives, USBs, or the cloud. It will probably run much faster once you do.

Anything can happen, and it's quick when it does! Make your way through *The BIG Checklist* system and habits to ensure you're prepared for the worst.

3 - Charting your Digital Life

One of the best ways for me to see my complete digital life was to create a digital life list. This list, or chart, will be your guide through the process of digital decluttering. I will help you find all of your digital clutter and then provide ideas to help you shuffle it around to make the best use of your digital space. It is all like a complicated game of Tetris.

You have dropped digital breadcrumbs all over the virtual world, and now it's time to follow them by compiling all of your digital spaces together. Start by creating a list or a map of your digital adventures so far.

❑ Check each of one of your cloud storage options, how many GBs are available to use, and how much you are utilizing.

Start a digital note and do a quick brainstorm of all the digital accounts you have. You can also use a plain piece of paper and a pen for this task. You won't remember them all in your first go, and that's okay. It's all about getting started, and as you move about picking up all those old breadcrumbs, you'll remember other paths you've visited. You'll be using your list to keep track of your progress and mark your wins.

❑ Check each external hard drive, USB, and SD card for the capacity of data and the amount of data still available.

Separate your business versus your personal devices. Mark or place the accounts in order of priority for your lifestyle. You will use this to track your progress and mark your victories.

Accounting for your hardware in your list will be a good way to either write a good outline or create a good mind map through loads of your digital life. Do a complete inventory of your devices; you'll also need to know your physical devices' memory capacity.

Your hardware is the bones of your digital life.
Don't forget the quantity and quality of your hardware as you put together your digital life list. Each piece helps make your digital adventures possible and will either be an asset or a liability in your quest to declutter.

Remember, your Apple TV, Roku Box, or PlayStation are each pieces of hardware that are an aspect of your digital life and need to be properly maintained and accounted for.

Your brainstorming list will initially grow as you move through your digital life. It will shrink and resize in various areas as you declutter and reorganize along the way. Create a minimalist black-and-white list in a spreadsheet (it doesn't need to be fancy) and write down which device has programs you need to declutter.

I've included a sample spreadsheet of my original starting line stats to show you one way to keep track of your numbers and data storage. You'll find it in Appendix I. Assessing the value of having various accounts and consolidating digital assets will give a better view of what should be reallocated or deleted. It will give you the confidence to straight up delete detritus you have accumulated over the past years, or even the past decades! The numbers on your digital life list are your starting line stats.

Every quest needs a map!
Mind mapping is another way in which to take notes. Hazel Wagner, Ph.D., states in her TED Talk that mind mapping is a free form

way of taking notes about what you remember. It's little more than keywords, short phrases, and a sketch, but most of all it's about the connections we have within our own brains from one description to the next.

It works more like the mind works and helps us remember through movement, known as kinesthetic memory. It is usually created on a single paper spread so we can read the keywords and phrases that we have written. We start with the topic or goal. It is from this topic written out in the middle of the page that our notes are then added to it going out radially.

I've included a mind-mapping example of digital clutter in Appendix II. You may prefer to create a mind-mapping-designed list. You have ignored your bread crumbs along the way and need to grab your colorful markers and do a fun bit of mind mapping as you remember where all of your cyber adventures have taken you. List your systems on a graph and map them like it's a fantasy quest map. Use your fun metallic pens with ink of one color and glitter in a sparkling accent color. Create a combination of both; create a list that works for you.

Your digital life, in list form or mind-mapped, will be your guide for your decluttering quest. There are a lot of paths that you have taken and accounts you have created, and it will tax your memory. That's okay; you'll stumble upon a few of your less trodden pathways and you'll add them to the list as you move through your journey to declutter.

You'll remember accounts that you left because they suddenly changed their features for the worse or altered their terms of service, leaving a few digital assets there that you really should collect before canceling the account.

Whichever way you choose to put together your digital life list, get started with the following series of prompts and questions.

For each email account you own, take note:
❑ Record how much data in GB you are allocated.

❑ Note how many emails you have in each account.
❑ List how much data you are currently using in each account and how much data you have left.
❑ Mark its cost. Is it free? If you pay for it, what are the pricing tiers?
❑ Separate personal versus business accounts.
❑ Remember your "throwaway" email account - Whenever you are asked for an email account to receive discounts and special notices from stores, this is the one you give them so their emails don't clog up your primary email account. This needs a good cleanout once in a while. The good news if you use an email service such as Gmail is that you have additional online services along with the email. There is 15GB of total storage space, including your emails, to use for free. Be sure to include these GBs as available storage as part of your digital life list.
❑ Finding all of your email accounts - Additional email accounts to add are your one-time hobby or event emails, the community workshop email account that you manage, etc. When I started taking note of my accounts, I was down to five email accounts, which seemed low. It turned out that I missed a couple in my initial decluttering session, so I added them along the way during my decluttering process.

Note your photography and video accounts:
❑ Note each cloud account that contains your digital photos.
❑ Mark each physical device in which you store your images and video, such as your smartphone, external hard drives, SD cards, USBs, CDs, etc.
❑ Mark the total available data space on each.
❑ Include the amount of data used. This will help you determine where to balance them. Make conscious decisions regarding their locations and long-term storage.

PRO Tip: I have created an index note in Google Keep for each of my Gmail accounts. This way I can easily see the inventory of digital assets I store in each.

How BIG is your digital life? If you're reading this book, it's probably a monster like mine was! Think beyond the usual, such as emails, photos, and your desktop. Every single thing you have ever needed a login for is part of your digital life—everything from ordering a pair of shoes to an old LiveJournal account, from your pet's chip to filing your taxes!

The size of your digital life is probably much larger than you suspect. You may think you have 30 - 40 accounts, but in reality, you probably have way over 100 accounts!

Upon accumulating your digital life list or map, you'll initially think you have everything listed, but know that you will likely remember two, three, five, or even ten more accounts that you have collected. Despite having all those accounts, there is probably that one more email account to consider, like that Garmin workout account or that digital sheet music account.

Your list will initially grow as you find these extra accounts. Don't worry . . . it will begin to get smaller and more manageable as you declutter, rearrange, and right-size your digital life.

I've provided a brief list with examples to prompt you. The smallest and oldest accounts will be the easiest to make quick, executive decisions regarding.

- ❑ Banking, Accounting, Finance, Taxes
- ❑ Books - Creation of
- ❑ Books - Consumption of
- ❑ Business
- ❑ Entertainment - Creation of; YouTube, Twitch, Patreon
- ❑ Entertainment - Consumption of; Netflix, Sports
- ❑ Faith
- ❑ Fitness & Health - Garmin, Fitbit
- ❑ Food & Drink
- ❑ Games - Animal Crossing, Candy Crush
- ❑ Lifestyle/Hobbies
- ❑ Magazines & Newspapers; Feedly
- ❑ Medical
- ❑ Messaging Apps - LINE, Whats App
- ❑ Music - Creation of

- ❏ Music - Consumption of
- ❏ Note-taking apps - Evernote, OneNote
- ❏ Photography - Photoshop, Light Meter App
- ❏ Reference - Language apps
- ❏ Shopping
- ❏ Social Networking - Do you have more than one Twitter or Instagram account? What about older, abandoned accounts, such as an old Tumblr account?
- ❏ Travel and Navigation
- ❏ Utilities
- ❏ Video
- ❏ Weather
- ❏ Website - Blog, WordPress, Squarespace

Please remember that it took you years, even decades, to accumulate the digital life you have. It takes time to slow the accumulation, and then reverse its course. Be patient with yourself; using many small steps—slow and steady—will allow you to tackle this huge project and gain control of your digital mess.

Referring to this list will be a great lookback to see your progress. It will likely be an up-and-down effort throughout your journey. This is a marathon, not a sprint, with rest days and hard hills to climb, but you will be making progress overall. Good habits take time to stick. Your digital life numbers are your starting line stats, which can be used to track your progress and celebrate your victories over your digital clutter.

4 - Starting Line Stats

Put your toes up to the line; this is where your decluttering journey begins.

You've compiled your digital life list in Chapter 3, but now, what do you do with this list? This is the nitty-gritty list of the digital clutter in which you need to take command. You will come back to this list again and again and will do so in waves. You've marked the numbers so you can track your progress. Mark the total MBs of folders and the total amount of GBs and TBs of data space you rent or own.

Think of your digital assets as if they are currently in messy warehouse storage units. You rent or own a lot of storage units—small ones, large ones, and ones in various locations throughout your town, your country, or even the world. Usually you rent your cloud space units and you own your devices, USBs, external hard drives, etc. Most of your digital assets are unevenly distributed, with a large warehouse unit sitting nearly empty with few items while a small unit is full to bursting with warning emails being sent incessantly.

Knowing the total amount of data storage available to you will help you efficiently redistribute your data.

You have some data in the cloud and other data on a tablet. The data stored only on your tablet is vulnerable to personal emergencies such as fire, flooding, or theft, but the data stored in the cloud is still accessible from other locations after your emergency has passed. However, data in the cloud is also susceptible to other problems such as a data breach or its own fire or hurricane risks. Data saved in the cloud is literally your information on someone else's computer that you are renting. Take care to save your data where you feel most comfortable keeping it. If you lay awake at night worrying about it, you may need to move it to a different type of storage, or multiple storage spaces. You may also want to stop relying on free storage . . . it invariably becomes a pay option.

The nitty-gritty stats of where my digital decluttering journey began are listed on a spreadsheet in Appendix I. You'll see I needed to ask myself several questions. Let's go through some of the clutter I had hiding on my computer.

I have multiple email accounts, and I needed to list each of them separately. I like that I can mark great progress in my digital life list by decluttering accounts with the smallest number of emails, then deleting them. Then I have fewer email accounts to keep track of on a regular basis.

Personal Emails:
Email #1 - 1503
Email #2 - 2802
Email #3 - 117

Business Emails:
Email #4 - 14
Email #5 - 317
Email #6 - 0 (I may delete this email, although I may keep it as a cloud space option because it has 15GB of data space available. In the meantime, it's just an empty parking space)

Do I really need this many email accounts? They each serve a purpose, but is that reason enough to keep them going? My life has changed since opening a couple of these accounts and it may be best to either cancel or utilize their forwarding and storage features.

Photos - 4,390, plus an unknown backlog from an old smartphone. Don't forget about the backlog from other devices. I had to ask myself, "Do I really want or need all of these old documents and photos?"
If I set a goal of editing or deleting 100 photos per day, that comes to a total of 36,500 photos per year! I'm sure I can delete at a pace greater than I accumulate with only 4300 photos.

Video files - 131. Video files consume a huge amount of data, even if they are the short, less-than-30-second videos I enjoy creating. When I'm running out of data, the first place I look is in my videos. Do you have photographs and video in multiple accounts such as Flickr, Google Photos, or Adobe Creative Cloud? I know I have duplicates amongst the multiple accounts because when I upload a photo for editing and use on my website, I'm worried about deleting the original photograph or video. And then there are the various versions that I've edited. Ultimately, do I really need all of these versions? Probably not. Keeping the original and a .PSD version should be enough for my limited needs.

There is no known unlimited and permanently free data storage space, so shop around for the best value for your needs. SmugMug has various levels of storage and pay options, and so does Adobe's Creative Cloud. Even a smaller option of 100GB is still a LOT of data storage. A friend of mine has been caught out multiple times on unlimited storage accounts that suddenly become pay for play.

That will give you a small taste of what I worked through. There was a lot of clutter that I had floating around inside my devices, as I am sure you do as well.

I looked at how much music I owned and on which devices it was stored. In addition to music I listen to, I had sheet music scattered in several different places. Most of it was in the cloud and some was specifically downloaded to a device in case I didn't have an internet connection when I wanted to practice.

Following my music theme led me to discover other bits of my digital life, like the tuning apps, the electronic sheet music accounts, and the metronome app that goes along with being a musician.

As I took control of my digital life, I stumbled across other piles of clutter and added each one to my starting line stats. This is going to be a long journey, I realized, one with progress and missteps, lessons learned the hard way, and new options available to make things easier as I make my way through it all.

Put your toes up to the line and take the challenge. Start your quest for an uncluttered digital life. Regularly keep track of your digital decluttering. Reward your progress. Update the numbers on the digital life list you created, and create columns for each week or month. Give yourself a gold star for all of your progress, each time.

Some of you are good with knowing that the simple numbers themselves are dropping. A simple line graph or colorful bar graph may be the motivation you need to see your progress. Some of you would really like to see a physical reward such as jellybeans in a bowl.

It's okay to fall off the proverbial wagon. Life happens. It's jumping back into the habit as soon as possible that will ensure you accomplish your goal.

5 - Those Are Some Overwhelming Numbers!

No one wakes up in the morning deciding they are going to make the biggest mess of things possible. Yet, here we are with an overwhelming mess. So, why do we fail? Why do we procrastinate on something that will benefit us in the long term? You usually have such high aspirations to clean up after yourself! So, how did you get here with this jumbled pile of clutter? Why is it that we fail absolutely miserably at keeping the clutter at bay?

❑ More clutter is coming in than you're able to declutter - Being out of sight also hides exactly how big your pile of digital clutter really is. A few MBs here, a bunch of GBs there and suddenly you are staring at a Terabyte or two.

❑ You have no time - You are losing so much time searching for your lost files. If you had a good system in place, a good workflow, you could save a lot of time properly filing your assets rather than searching for them. We are living in an age when business is moving faster and faster and expectations are pushing higher and higher, so the reality is that you need to be even more organized. But you feel there is no time. Between personal, work, and family issues, you got behind and just haven't been able to catch up. You feel like you're behind the eight ball.

❑ Poor habits - My poor digital habits, such as letting vacation photos sit forever on my phone, came from my out-of-sight, out-of-mind mentality. I wasn't physically tripping over my digital clutter. There was no particular stench like you would smell from a pile of workout clothes, and there were no rumbling stomachs to feed, so it was extremely easy to ignore my digital clutter until I needed to find a specific photograph or document.

The best way I now keep on top of what will easily become a massive clutter pile is to schedule the time to organize the clutter. If I don't put it into my calendar, it does not get done.

Consider vacation photos, for example. If I have time during vacation, such as at an airport, I may go through a couple of photographs, but I usually prefer to stay in the moment. The bulk of my photos are edited about a week after the vacation at home. I specifically set aside several hours or more depending on how many photos and videos I have. You know you'll need a block of time to go through the photographs at some point, either now or some ambiguous time in the future. Schedule the time. Write it into your calendar, before you even go on your trip. Schedule the editing time for a time after you've rested and jet lag has subsided. Then you can create a fun video or a photo book for later.

I do the same right after a big project is completed. I schedule the time in my calendar to do a reset. A reset is the time I need to file or delete the various documents necessary for future reference on a project. If I need to go back, I have an organized file ready to answer questions and resolve issues.

❑ Computers are confusing - Is organizing your files simply out of your skillset at the moment? Can't keep up with the program changes and feel like a Luddite preferring the analog life? How does one go about moving all these files around? You thought you deleted all those photos, so why does your computer run slowly? I can show you a couple of steps to help clear things up, but your favorite search engine will be your friend.

I have learned a lot about my computer and peripheral devices through my digital decluttering process, and I am glad I took the time to do so. I feel more in command of my computer and other devices for having done so. Your new knowledge will add value to your computer. It will open up capabilities you didn't know you had available to you. Most of it is about learning basic functions, so jump in and learn!

PRO Tip: The current mess of your digital assets took years to accumulate, and it will take time to declutter and organize it. It also took a long time to declutter your home after years of accumulation. Be persistent. Keep going back to another item on your list. There is usually one tough corner where you have the most clutter, whereas another area doesn't apply to you at all. Always return to your most cluttered areas. Your dogged determination to keep organizing will be worth the effort!

I have found the following Mark Twain quote very motivating: "If it's your job to eat a frog, it's best to do it first thing in the morning. And if it's your job to eat two frogs, it's best to eat the biggest one first."

I choose three main tasks I'd like to accomplish each day in order to feel like I have had a good day. At least once each week, I need to do an annoying task I try to put off doing. But I do have my rewards, and depending upon the amount of stress I felt it took for me to complete the task, I am sure to reward myself at the end.

Utilize what is available to you and those which you feel most comfortable using. Yes, each solution has its own problems, but that is why you don't put all your eggs into one basket. Sure, you have files backed up to iCloud by your Apple devices, but having your most important items also in an external hard drive or with another cloud service (such as Google Drive) will help you worry less about loss.

Your digital footprint is huge. It's okay if you choose not to make it smaller. Make mindful choices about what to keep, move, or delete. As we continue to declutter, we often find space to digitize more of our paper records or transform our vacation photographs into a fun video. It's about the best organization possible for your digital needs. It's about streamlining your system for ease of use and to ensure you are making the most of your digital assets in combination with the digital storage you have available.

You are not alone, and you can reach digital minimalism.
❑ Set your long-term and short-term goals - Mark what your long-term, monthly, or yearly goals are from the beginning. As Stephen Covey said, "Start with the end in mind." Then mark in your monthly and weekly goals to make the yearly goal happen.

For example, let's say you have 7200 photographs to declutter. Start with the end goal of your photographs being decluttered in six months, which is 180 days. Can you reasonably declutter 40 photographs each day or 280 photographs each week for the next six months? Complete the small daily and weekly actions and the long-term goal will be accomplished. Be sure to mark your end goal in your starting line stats. Adjust your goals as necessary throughout your decluttering process.

Solutions are available; you just need to know where to find them. There is a wide range of systems and solutions available to you to keep your digital clutter under control—from free solutions to very expensive options depending on your lifestyle needs.

❑ Can you delete enough data to reduce your storage needs and save money? Or can you redistribute files to make the most of what you are already paying for? Be careful with how much you place on a monthly pay site, such as Adobe Creative Cloud. You can utilize 100GB with their monthly plan, but if you run into a financial emergency and are suddenly unable to pay for the storage space, you may lose all your data. Don't stress; there is hope, and there are solutions and systems available to make your decluttering job easier. Start streamlining the process. Do you have any small, older accounts you can cull quickly?

❑ You may tackle each section in whichever order you'd like. I loved the Choose Your Own Adventure books as a child. What will your path be on your quest towards a digitally organized life?

❑ Start by searching the Apple or Microsoft forums - Here you'll find your most immediate and up-to-date solutions. Sometimes there are built-in solutions to help with decluttering. There are apps such as CleanMyMac X which is an example of one such option to help scan and declutter your files in addition to searching for viruses and malware.

❑ Ask your search engine - You are likely not the first person to have questions, so you're likely to find several answers available to you with each question you ask in your favorite search engine. Sometimes it takes a couple of guesses to find the correct computer jargon to ask the right question that will provide a good, workable answer.

❑ YouTube - There are several YouTube videos that have been invaluable to me. They opened my eyes to many solutions that I wasn't aware of. I found this most useful when I needed to research external drive solutions, USBs, and card readers.

❑ Connect with your friends - At least one of them will have already encountered the same problems as you are having with your computer. I have monthly and sometimes weekly working accountability and admin meetings with friends, and I find that with just a quick question, there is at least one person who has a quick solution to my problem, or else they can direct me towards a solution I would have had difficulty finding on my own. Then I'm able to jump right back into my work and finish up with that goal for the day. There is always a friend who has been where you are now. Call them, text them, or email them to help with small computer questions.

❑ Create a system - Many of you do not have a good system in place to enjoy an organized digital life. Oh, you try with a random file here and there, but the speed and amount in which you accumulate information is taking over the time in which you'd properly create systems to sort your files. Continually adding apps brings in another new dimension to your files. And the updates . . . oh, the repeated updates! It may not be apparent immediately, but as you dig deeper into your computer's capabilities and options, patterns will start to emerge, and you can then begin to create a system that works for your lifestyle.

PRO Tip: Monthly Stats - Chart your progress! It's great to see when we make progress towards our goals. The physical manifestation of our efforts is a helpful motivator, and putting it into a line or bar graph or just seeing the numbers get smaller is great.

6 - Three BIG Steps to Jump-start Your Decluttering Process

1. Clear Off Your Desktop:
Each morning, the shopkeepers here in Japan clean the sidewalk in front of their shops before opening. It's a brief task that includes a quick sweep and a spray down with a hose or a bucket. It's a ritual sweeping of their space, a ritual cleansing. I found myself choosing to sweep out my studio space each morning, reclaiming my space for the day and owning my physical environment as a ritual start to the day. I have added this small, ritual sweeping to my digital world as well.

❑ Clean your screen - I keep the screen cloth in a convenient location to do so before each morning use. Physical cleaning of your devices is a way to take command of your physical space and your property, including your digital space.

❑ Power Up! - Pushing the power button on your device is the start of laying claim to your digital space. Currently, your computer is like walking into that one messy room in your home or that messy closet that is a dumping ground for items we just aren't sure where else to place. It brings a distressing sigh whenever you open the door, and you just close the door after tossing yet another item there. You're paralyzed and overwhelmed by the clutter. The same goes for your computer's desktop. A pile of documents, photographs, digital instruction books, tax forms, and other miscellaneous flotsam and jetsam of your digital life is just glaring at you.

Do you dream of opening your laptop, pressing the power button, and seeing an unobscured wallpaper photo of you snowboarding last winter? Or one of the fun times your family had at the BBQ for your birthday? Or your sweet, fluffy pet? Best of all, your computer will often boot up faster than before you decluttered your desktop!

The very practical reason to keep your computer's desktop clean and decluttered is that too many files and too large of files on your desktop will slow your computer. It will be slow to boot up and it'll be slow to close down. It will also slow your workflow as your current working file will drown amongst the sea of distracting files on your desktop.

Treat your desktop like a train station platform. Files are frequently coming and going on your desktop as you work, then moving on to their destinations. When you close down for the night, there shouldn't be any files left on the platform.

Decluttering our desktop will allow you to breathe easier from the moment you turn on your computer. Each time you start up our computer from now on, you will both see and feel the difference a big declutter will have on your well-being.

It took me several timed work sessions to fully clear my desktop off, as I had a lot of decisions that needed to be made:
❑ Trash it.
❑ File it.
If I kept it: ❑ Find or create a home for this file.

❑ Schedule your decluttering work sessions - Doing a desktop clear-out can be a daunting task and may take several scheduled work sessions to complete. It's a good time to start a regular habit of decluttering the day's accumulation. Taking command of your desktop space will show you how much control you have over your digital life.

❑ Separate work files versus personal files.

❑ Separate your files as you would organize them in your real-life filing system, such as by theme, date, or the person in the photographs.

❑ Delete duplicates.

❑ Reward yourself! - When you have finished removing all the files from your desktop, reward yourself with a new desktop wallpaper! Create a restful place for your eyes, such as a beach scene, a family photo, or a Zen garden. Your work computer could display project goals or a motivational phrase as a good way to jump-start your day.

❑ Bonus action - Curate the apps in your dock. Improve your workflow by moving apps you often use into your dock or taskbar and remove apps you rarely use. In the systems preferences section of your computer, you can choose various options to improve your desktop experience.

2. Empty Your Downloads Folder:
Downloads folder? What downloads folder? Yes, sadly, that was me. It's supposed to be a single folder where all of the items you have downloaded end up on your computer. In reality, for me, it's that dead-end road in the backwoods where everyone does their illegal dumping, a very unfortunate, scary pile of garbage. It becomes a whole heap of different kinds of files mish-mashed into a single folder. Several years of downloads accumulated before I understood how the system worked with regards to downloads.

The accumulation easily added up to a large amount of valuable data space. Decluttering by placing some items in the correct files, and lots of deleting of files, has freed up several GBs of digital space better utilized elsewhere.

Most of the photographs and videos had already been placed in other files. Some had long since been deleted, and I did not realize there was still a copy in the downloads folder. The same was true with many of the documents; I already had the file in another location, and the computer programming chose to keep an original file in the downloads.

Did I really need the instructions for the crazy foldable traveling bicycle hex wrench thingy anymore? No. Delete! Buried in my downloads folder, I even found an "about downloads" PDF file.

I did need to do some research to learn what I was looking at. What are the .dmg, .exe, and .pkg files? Adobe Flash Player installer? ZoomusInstaller.pkg? Firefox.dmg? Garmin.exe?

Is it okay for you to delete them?
The long and short of it is that it depends. Most likely, yes. However, if you ever need or want to reinstall that program for whatever reason, you will need that file again. Most apps can be completely reloaded from the internet with no problems, but for some older programs, that may not be possible. If you are unsure, placing them in a preferred file location for later use if necessary may be the best choice for you.

❏ Create your own "Just in Case" folder - The files you place in this folder are the ones you don't feel comfortable deleting yet. Mine has a few miscellaneous files. I'm still not sure what they are; they don't take up much data space, and I'm too afraid I'll need them at a later point. Maybe I'll delete these mysterious downloads in the next wave.

3. Update Your Sleep Settings:
This may seem like an odd way to digitally declutter one's life, but good sleep is vital. It makes the day's challenges a little easier to handle and a little less stressful to find that extra five minutes to delete a few more emails.

Insomnia affects approximately a third of people in the US. We need good sleep as it is vital for our executive functioning and our ability to think clearly and make good decisions. The causes of insomnia are many, with our smartphones adding yet another reason for our lack of proper sleep. According to the Sleep Foundation, "Sleep feeds creativity, synthesizes new ideas, and leads you to 'ah-ha' moments. Research shows that we need good sleep to feed our high-level, innovative thinking and problem-solving abilities."

Each day you go to bed and have trouble sleeping, you spend too much time swiping through social media or you are awakened by mobile notifications. Simply needing to check the time on your smartphone will lead to distracted sleep.

Today, before you crawl into bed, exhausted, there are several steps you can take to have your digital life support better sleep.

❏ Set "Do Not Disturb" - Discover which of your smartphone's "Do Not Disturb" options will help lock in your sleep time. Schedule "Do Not Disturb" settings for your preferred sleep or nap time with the "Allow phone calls from…" option to help you rest easy so that you will still be available for an emergency.

❏ Reduce screen brightness - Bedtime functions with a dimmer lock screen will allow you to see the time but not be jolted awake by the bright light.

❏ Set your smartphone's screen to night mode, which reduces the amount of blue light emitted, to fall asleep faster. I am a voracious reader and have always fallen asleep reading a book from the time I learned to read. Any other dark-mode options in your eReader apps will work as well, such as a black background with white letters. This will also save your battery power.

❏ Do you like to have someone read a book to you? Try Audible or free Open Source classics. From Jane Austen to Edgar Allen Poe, there are a lot of great classics available. Well, maybe a horror writer such as Poe isn't the best choice right before sleep.

❏ Sounds to fall asleep by - Would you like to fall asleep to the soothing sounds of warm tropical ocean waves? Or what about white noise? There are a plethora of apps and ASMR information available to help you fall asleep. Autonomous Sensory Meridian Response, or ASMR, according to The Sleep Foundation, is described as,

> "...a feeling of euphoric tingling and relaxation that can come over someone when he or she watches certain videos or hears certain sounds."

The resultant feelings can bring on relaxation, helping to bring on sleep more easily. It's often soundtracks from simple, comfortable settings like a library, the rain, or the breeze through summer leaves.

❑ Separate digital alarm clock - Should you obtain a separate alarm clock for when you need to check the time in the middle of the night? Just picking up your smartphone will prompt you to take a quick peek at your social media or the latest news, or to check on the markets in London. Do you need to go one step further and keep your phone out of the bedroom?

❑ Set the sleep timer on your television - Do you like to fall asleep with the television on simply to be awakened by it later in the night? Set a timer on your television, either within its own functions or with an attached timer to its plug-in.

❑ Sleep cycle apps - What you learn from these apps could help you sleep, or they could just be for fun to learn more about yourself. Sleep apps are still in the early stages and aren't always very accurate. Keep the one that does help and delete the rest. Only keep the one that works for you.

❑ Wake up! - Set your alarm for each day of the week for the optimal time. Choose the sound you want to awaken to. Have you been able to use the information from the sleep cycle app to get more restful sleep? There are quite a few studies out there that show the benefits of waking up without an alarm. If you consistently go to bed at a reasonable time, you'll find you wake up on your own and feel far more rested. Once your body is used to waking up at the same time every day, there is little need for an alarm.

By completing these three BIG items to launch your decluttering journey, your computer is likely running a bit faster, has a bit more available data space, and you are on your way to a more relaxing decluttering session.

7 - Know Your Computer: System Preferences

Your System Preferences, also known as the Settings app, is your device's mastermind behind the curtain. The system preferences is where you go to improve your digital experience with your computer. There is a lot that you can control in this section, from accessibility options to connecting to your printer to the cloud to which users you will give permission to use your computer.

My digital decluttering journey has helped me learn about many of the features and benefits of my devices I had no idea were available. The lessons I learned have made my devices more valuable.

❏ Update the software - Before going through and changing your preferences, check for software updates. I'm not an early adopter of new updates. I usually wait a couple of days until the bugs are worked out. Then I will download the update and enjoy the new features on my devices.

Each time I bring home a shiny new computer I am so excited I jump right into downloading my preferred programs and visiting my favorite websites. I've researched the RAM, the screen clarity, the graphics card, and which accessories I need, such as the latest whizzbang widget, so I just assume I know my computer.

My current eight-year-old laptop was in my possession for almost three years before I chose to go through its system preferences section by section. I learned so much about this amazing piece of machinery and its capabilities that it felt shiny and new to me again. Software updates through the years make going through your systems settings important to get the most for your money.

❏ Declutter your systems - This is probably the easiest part of the whole decluttering process. The answers are usually simple on/off, limited multiple choice, or slider options. It's organized in such a way that it makes a checklist unnecessary. Click on each file one by one along the rows, read through the options as you go, and choose from what your computer says your options are. You'll be able to see if you want to make any changes.

Since my original purchase and many software updates later, I'm now able to enjoy dark mode on my laptop and night mode on my phone. And that really annoying issue I had with the disappearing scroll bars? Gone! One checkmark in the correct little box in a systems file and my digital experience was once again smooth and comfortable.

❏ Manage your notifications - The most immediate, daily impact you can do is to manage your notifications. Decide who you want to hear from regularly and who should not demand your attention anymore.

Other areas I've made setup changes in are the multiple languages keyboards, accessibility settings, and deletion of some cookies.

You've cleared off the files cluttering your desktop in Chapter 6 . . . are you happy with the new wallpaper image you chose to set the mood you want when you power up your computer each day?

Most of the options presented need no action. Some features have never been used and still have no place in my life. But if there is even one option that makes your digital experience smoother, it will be worth the effort.

PRO Tip: Have multiple working browsers at the ready. Not all programs work well with every browser, and switching comfortably between Safari, Firefox, and Chrome is important. Keep your preferred browsers ready to use and the software up to date—especially the plug-ins in Chrome.

8 - Digital Storage Units: Right-Size Your Options

There are three different ways in which your digital assets can be stored:
❑ Cloud services
❑ Device storage
❑ External storage (SD cards, external hard drives, USBs, CDs, etc.)

How much digital storage do you already own or have access to? How much digital storage do you need? Check your digital life list; you should have most of the answer already compiled. Each of these storage options can help you even out the workload in one area if moved to another. Keep going with your inventory of each of your storage options and see where you need to have more storage. In some cases, you can cancel that small charge per month for the extra storage you purchased in a panic.

Referring to your digital life list, you will now be able to manage your storage options and how much more (or less) you need. You have gone through all your photos and have determined how much storage you have and approximately how much storage you will need.

This is also a good time to assess how much more you need and take the time to research your best options as you can now clearly see what exactly you need to store, for how long, and how you will need to access it. Is it compatible with your home computer systems? Will it fit with the workflow you have in your business?

Assign cloud accounts or hard drives to specific devices or projects and specify their purpose. Can you make adjustments that will save you money? Check pricing options on the various hard drive and cloud storage options when you are making decisions about rearranging your storage and data options. Is an external hard drive a better option through a one-time purchase instead of purchasing cloud storage in perpetuity?

When comparing cloud storage versus your devices versus external storage, realize that data backup options vary, with each option having pros and cons.

Cloud storage:
This seems the most convenient option, and it's not very expensive unless you need a lot of storage. It's my favorite minimalist option, as long as bits of cords and hardware aren't lying around . . . and there aren't any, right? But the reality is that you are simply storing your data on someone else's computer. Its convenience is unparalleled for accessing almost anywhere in the world where you have an internet connection.

❑ How much storage do you have in your various cloud storage options from Google, Dropbox, iCloud, etc.? Which files can be shuffled around at this moment to keep from seeing "Your cloud storage is almost empty" multiple times each day?

I had a huge video on my iPad's iMovie app, and it was seriously limiting my ability to work on creating other videos. I often hit the ceiling on my iCloud data, but I have plenty of spare cloud data on other accounts. Choosing not to increase my iCloud storage—in other words, choosing not to pay for more cloud storage when I already have plenty in another area—I moved that large video file, the annoying messages have stopped, the headache is gone, and I now have 7GB of additional data space available.

Gmail provides 15GB of cloud storage per email, along with additional Google programs online, and somehow over the years I have accumulated several Gmail addresses to handle different areas of my life from personal to family to business.

Adobe Creative Cloud provides 100GB for subscribers, which seems like a lot, but when you are working in digital videos, those GBs get eaten away fast! Creating fun family vacation videos in Adobe is a great idea if you are comfortable with the software, but long-term storage is best on an external hard drive. Additionally, if you are regularly working in the Adobe environment, you'll need that space for current projects.

Some of you are in daily conflict with storage as you receive messages that you are near your cloud storage limit. You may discover that a forgotten account will be able to help with the overload. Best of all, you should start looking at what you truly need to keep and what can be moved to the trash.

Computer Device Storage:
When you buy a computer, it comes with a certain amount of storage on the device and it usually comes with a certain amount of cloud storage as well. Data stored on your device is the most convenient to use but can be limiting in size. For some, it is enough, but for many, we need to utilize additional storage options.

The strongest reasons to not keep important files only on your devices is because they are easily lost, stolen, or damaged.

A device like your smartphone is with you always, but it can easily be damaged, lost, or stolen, or it can suddenly quit working due to a bad software update or because it has outlived its parts' capabilities. Life expectancy is sometimes hard to determine considering warranties are only for a few years depending on the device. My laptop is eight years old and not very fast, but it's a workhorse that gets the job done, knock on wood. I'm prepared if it stops working at any time. My smartphone is over five years old. I'd love to get a new one, but this one keeps on ticking, knock on wood again. So while devices are very expensive, they can become a very inexpensive product for their productivity with longevity.

External device storage:
Let's consider external hard drive options. They are in your possession at all times, leaving you 100% responsible for your own data. Although, just like any computer device, they do not last forever. Think of floppy disks and CDs. They can get damaged, lost, or stolen, and you'll lose all your data. It happens. Keeping external drives means equipment and extra cords, but you have access to your data as long as you have electricity for your computer. Solid State Drives are large enough to hold a huge amount of data, such as 5TB, yet small enough to be extremely convenient to carry around.

❑ USBs are also small and very handy for carrying around, packing for an emergency, and transferring files from one computer to another. I don't have a printer and am thrilled to be able to put the few items I do print onto a USB and take them to be printed for a reasonable price and a lot less frustration than owning a printer! Same for SD cards.

In conclusion, which backup storage option is right for you and your information?

It is the storage option that allows you to sleep at night.

There are some documents and old family photos I have saved in three different places as I would worry if they were only saved in one place, called dual or triple redundancy. Consider how you would feel if you lost your next great novel, client proposal, or important tax forms. There are no right or wrong answers when it comes to how you choose to save your most valued digital assets. It's better to be safe than sorry and back up, back up, back up those important documents!

❑ Back up your digital assets - Write it in your schedule to do the backups or set up an automatic reminder to take regular action.

While cloud storage backups are usually automatically done in the background, external storage devices are only as good as the last time you backed up your information.

PRO Tip: Captive Decluttering - The most painless time I spend digitally decluttering is during what I call captive decluttering. It's the time we spend while trapped, waiting at the doctor's office until we are called. It's the time we spend waiting for a friend who is late to meet you at the neighborhood coffee shop, or that really, really long wait at the DMV. Waiting, waiting, waiting . . . how much time do we spend waiting each week?

Make this waiting time your time. How much of that time could be utilized to digitally declutter? After checking for messages that need your immediate attention, open your photo app, and start decluttering them. So many meetings don't start right on time. Arriving on time for many meetings brings about several minutes of decluttering opportunity. File or delete work emails as you wait for the others to arrive.

You can really make headway if each time you absent-mindedly move to go on your socials, you instead use this captive time for organizing your files or decluttering more photos. Selecting groups of photos and creating smaller albums will allow you to more easily achieve multiple smaller goals. This is a great time to create those smaller batches.

9 - Accountability Team

Every quest needs a team!
Friends, partners, and teams working towards the same dreams help push each other, support each other, and provide regular check-ins along with much-needed exchanges of information. A mind-numbing marathon task such as digital decluttering can be made so much easier by decluttering with friends. Same as athletic training or weight-loss programs, finding a supportive partner or team makes the tough days much easier to complete.

❑ Set up a regular check-in time with your accountability partners. Share at least one goal you plan to accomplish before the next check-in session.

❑ Work sessions - A big part of my digital decluttering is based on my business activities in art, photography, and travels. In one of the accountability groups I participate in, we will get together to complete our admin work, the behind-the-scenes office work that keeps our businesses running smoothly. We each have our own knowledge bases depending upon our work and have found that a hurdle one person finds has often already been surmounted by another, and we can all quickly move forward with all of our work.

Good accountability partners have been proven to successfully work in creating a supportive team in reaching difficult, long-term goals.

❏ Don't be shy about asking. None of us had been worrying about how cluttered our homes were, and yet The Life-changing Magic of Tidying Up by Mari Kondo comes out and we begin bragging and video podcasting just how much clutter we are removing from our homes.

❏ Are you up to the challenge? - Meet your decluttering goals through challenges. What is your current challenge to yourself? Are you deleting at least 20 extra messages from your inbox each day? Or an additional 50? I recently saw a friend who had over 15,000 emails in their active email inbox. By active I mean the one they used daily, not a set-to-ignore junk email. 15,000 divided by 365 is 41 emails per day to have an empty inbox within a year. It's less than I expected, but still, a concerted effort needs to be made if he is to properly empty his inbox. These numbers are based on there being no additional accumulated emails. What will happen when the inbox is full? He may already be receiving stressful messages about how full his inbox is. One small habit change will bring all of it under control.

Make the challenge a contest of the percentage of emails decluttered each week or each month. Or measure success by the percentage of found GBs. Long-term, mind-numbing projects are the most difficult to complete on one's own.

❏ Resolve to jump back in each time you slack.

❏ Your goals are for a more relaxing digital experience, in both work and play.

You and your team need to be able to find all of your digital assets as quickly as possible, but you may be simply overwhelmed in your current situation. There are so many of you that I felt it important to put *The BIG Checklist* together.

Your goals are a more relaxing and streamlined work effort along with more fulfilling entertainment experiences. More control over your screen time gives back your control and command of your digital lives. You make decisions regarding the focus of your efforts and you make decisions regarding your time.

PRO Tip: Create a system of qualifications to keep on top of incoming clutter, starting with "No." Specify when, with whom (your accountability partner), and where you will regularly keep the hordes of clutter at bay. For example, when asked about taking a new online class, remind yourself and your accountability partners that you resolved not to take any new classes until you have taken the time to apply what you have learned in the other online classes you have taken. If you already know you love taking online classes, make the decision and the resolution before you encounter the question.

How often is best to do check-ins? Once per week with work and accountability partners and do it by percentages versus quantity regarding numbers of photographs, also. You are most likely to make your biggest gains and sweeping deletions in the first couple of weeks. Keep track and watch your starting line stat numbers go down. You could connect daily in the beginning as you see some of your biggest gains. For those of you who need to take small bites each day in your digital decluttering, you'll see your best gains in keeping track of your decluttering habits and checking in on a weekly basis.

10 - Emails & Good Habits

"Energy and persistence conquer all things." - Ben Franklin

Decluttering your email . . . how do you even begin to tackle this monster? Your emails grow at an exponential rate with no action on your part.

It took time to grow to 2500, or 15,000, or even over 30,000, and you receive daily messages that you are running out of space! It will take time to slow the snowball of accumulation and to properly file or delete that many emails while still managing the quantity coming in.

With the messages you've been receiving from your email provider, it is way past time to dig out the clutter. All too soon you will run out of space and no longer be able to receive any more messages or add any more digital assets to your services in conjunction with your email. You are looking for the quickest way to find the largest amount of data to delete.

"But wait," you ask, "what about all of my photos?" Photos take up a huge amount of our data space, but the only way the numbers of photos and videos grow is if you take the photos and capture the video in the first place. You have 100% control of it growing in quantity, whereas emails keep coming even while you are sleeping. I really feel there are quite a few tasks and habits that need to be taken care of first before diving into your photos. The habits learned and applied in this chapter are helpful and will apply throughout the rest of your decluttering process.

The extra time taken now to eliminate the stockpile of emails will become the extra time each day you will have to organize your photographs later. The photos aren't going anywhere, yet some emails do need personal attention as soon as possible, and many need to be deleted. So don't worry, your backlog of photos and videos will receive your full attention soon.

❏ Slow the avalanche - Tips to quickly delete a load of email clutter.

❏ Unsubscribe - Beginning with your older messages, it is good to see which messages you receive regularly yet never read. Ever. Unsubscribe from these emails, and then delete them permanently. These are the bloats that feel the best for me to delete.

❏ Filters: Set them up - Create filters to redirect emails to their correct folder, completely bypassing your inbox. Use filters to collate and delete all those sales or promotional emails and the several newsletters you receive.

❏ "Throwaway" email account - Redirect store sales and their digital brochure info to this email address. This is your garbage bin email account. It's easy enough to create, and you can literally set it and ignore it. If I don't read the messages within the first week, I don't ever go back to read them. By then the sales are over, the event has been done, and the sender has moved onto the next thing. There is too much business and other activities that come piling in for me to go back and look at them. When it gets full and you start to receive warnings, simply delete all the emails, and you've just taken the garbage out!

The further back in time the email is, the easier it is to determine which sales and which company's emails I will simply never read. Bulk deleting and unsubscribing is so refreshing! Your throwaway email account is easiest in which to delete and empty your inbox.

❏ Organize the emails you keep - Use the folder and file options within your email setup to organize your emails, or possibly send them to a note-taking app.

PRO Tip: Your inbox is not your to-do list!
I made this mistake for too long. It's a reactive way to conduct your business versus taking proactive actions. I used to keep emails for ongoing projects all in the inbox, as I needed to refer to them often and I didn't want to lose them. Sometimes projects last as long as six months, a year, or more, so I ended up with a massive number of emails. By the time I had moved onto the next projects, I simply needed those emails to get moved to a folder or deleted.

You have seven email accounts, so which one should you declutter first? You're looking at your digital life list and your seven different email accounts, all with varying degrees of clutter. Which do you move your attention to first?

❏ If you have an account you use daily and are repeatedly receiving messages that it is near or at its limit, this is your most urgent task.

❏ Next is the email account with the smallest amount of clutter - Deleting the oldest emails and having a greater perspective of its true importance or lack thereof will help you move them all into the trash that much faster.

❏ The largest emails will be the ones with attachments, so do a specific search for those. In Gmail, click on the arrow in the search box and check "has attachment." Now you can choose to properly file the emails and attachments or completely delete these largest emails.

Be decisive!
1. Keep it (create a folder in which to store it)
2. Move it to another data storage option
3. Delete it

❑ Go back in time to some of the oldest emails, the ones you know are not likely to be necessary any longer.

❑ Delete by sender - Using the 'Search' function, it's easy to collect and organize larger numbers of emails into batches for deletion or to then send them to subfolders. It's easier to declutter in smaller and smaller batches. This has helped me dump large numbers of emails quickly.

❑ Clean your inbox - Schedule a time to clean your inbox, like a workout to keep it fit. Do a solid culling of emails at least once per week.

❑ Choose the time of day to answer your emails - Scheduling the time to answer your emails ensures your focus on completing the task. Emails come in at all hours of day and night. You'll see when one needs an immediate answer and take appropriate action. Wait to answer all others until the scheduled time.

My scheduled time to answer emails is at noontime, and I tackle them as two different types.
❑ Easy emails only need quick answers with my response being easy and immediate.
❑ Difficult emails are ones I need to research my answer in greater detail that cannot be completed within the currently scheduled timeframe, like a new project proposal for example. Mark your schedule or add in your task manager when you will take a focused approach to complete the response required.

PRO Tip: For security, use a different email for communication versus logins.

❑ Professional email and newsletter - Many email programs will block mass emails for their customers, including newsletters they have signed up for. These are the same newsletters that your business relies on to communicate with your customers. This stops emails from popular newsletter-sending companies such as MailChimp from appearing in the recipient's inbox. It is recommended you have a specific business email address that is connected to your website domain. Do you need to connect your newsletter account with a business email for more effective newsletter delivery?

❑ Update your email signatures - For each of your professional and personal email accounts, be sure the email signature has the current information.

❑ Inbox zero - Is this a reasonable digital decluttering goal? Or is using the search function an adequate alternative to the perfect filing system.

I love the idea of the inbox zero system! What a relief to see only the emails you'd like to see and everything sorted just so at the end of each day. But do you need this intense level of email organization? When you stop using your email inbox as a to-do list, it isn't necessary to keep emails sitting in your inbox.

❑ Organizing emails into folders, or "Out of sight is out of mind" - I always felt that organizing my emails into folders was like cleaning your room by shoving everything under your bed when you were six—a mistake that would come back to haunt you.

One step of the inbox zero system is the tough suggestion of simply archiving it all. Maybe you'll need to do that at the end of each month, especially if you are cc'd on a lot of messages. It all sounds so dreamy, and as I read the process, I thought it would have me worrying about a lost email.

❑ Delete old email addresses from your contacts - Go through your email contacts list and see who can easily be deleted. Edit your contacts in each of your email accounts to ensure you have the correct email addresses. Cull the old emails that are just adding confusion to your email flow. Many may be outdated.

❑ Reconnect - After so many years, I found that I had accumulated a couple of different emails for the same friend, or I had a contact for a previous co-worker that had moved to a new company but was still a great contact in the same field to keep. Unsure which address is current? Ask! What a great way to keep in touch with them by asking the best email in which to do so. This is also a good time to update your own email address with others. If you have had email address changes since your last communication with them, now is the time to let them know so they can update their own email list.

Going through your contacts, the list can be good as you remember friends that you have drifted away from or who have moved away. If there are some you wish you had stayed in contact with, now is a good time to find their email and say, "Hi."

❑ Email Forgiveness Day - April 30th of each year. A recently created internet holiday from the podcast "Reply All" is another chance for you to reach out and reply to those emails you should have replied to a long time ago.

❑ Sent emails, too! - Declutter your sent emails. It isn't always all about the inbox. Don't forget about your sent items, which probably have a huge number of messages hanging out there having their own party with your data storage. So jump over there and make your way through the list.
Continue using the same process:
❑ Be decisive!
1. Keep it (create a folder in which to store it)
2. Move it to another data storage option
3. Delete it

❑ Filters, labels, flags, and folders for logical sorting systems - You can put together a beautifully ordered filing system if you'd like. All those labels of various kinds will help you be organized, but remember, you don't have to be super aggressive about every detail of the organization. If you have a few keywords available to you, the search option is often the most efficient.

❑ Behind the tabs - There is an option for email providers, such as Gmail, to automatically create specific "Promotions" or even "Junk" folders for newsletters to slide into, keeping your inbox looking otherwise uncluttered. Remember, this still counts against your data storage, so if they are going to a specific folder and you don't realize it, that really isn't helping you declutter.

❏ Digital file cabinet - Moving them to a folder system on the side is like placing them in a file cabinet for when you will need them next, such as at tax time. I do like to have several folders on the side in which to place important emails, such as messages with receipts and other important information I like to keep but need to keep out of my inbox. I am very much an out-of-sight, out-of-mind person, so these emails need to have a way for me to still see what they are (usually by subject), but I don't need to have them in my inbox.

❏ Delete. It's okay. Delete them. Be aggressive. These emails will go to your trash bin within your email system. Just putting items in the trash bin is not taking them out to the curb. At this time, the clock is ticking and they will stay in the trash bin for a specified period of time—such as two weeks or 30 days—before they are permanently deleted.

❏ Trash day - Delete your deleted emails! Right now, all of your deleted messages are probably sitting in your trash can, which is sitting next to the garage waiting for trash day. Trash day probably isn't for two weeks yet, so you can either wait to see if you suddenly start worrying about various messages you have aggressively deleted, or you can go in and delete all your trash to recapture your data storage space.

If you are deleting madly for the data space, you will need to go into the trash bin and click the empty button to get your data space ASAP.

This is where I find myself hitting delete, delete, delete over and over and over again. It can be a painfully long process and feel like you are making a sacrifice of your time and energy. The reduced stress of a clutter-free inbox will be worth it. Mass deleting was hard for me as I was concerned I would be deleting an important email in the batch.

❑ Archives folder - Where is that archives folder anyway? I had a hard time finding this folder in my Gmail account. Why is it that on my mobile app, my deleted Gmail messages go to archives instead of the trash? UGH! Go into your email settings and take a look at all of your options. You'll see settings that you can use to make your email experience easier.

❑ Deleting email accounts - Now that you have been tackling your piles of emails, you should have a better idea of where you stand with all of your email accounts. You know which ones you still need and which ones you know are just clutter in your life. Let go of the emails you don't want to deal with ever again. There will be less chance of more junk entering your digital life. If you aren't sure about deleting an email just yet, have it set up to forward to another email account. Keep track of its numbers and you'll get a better feeling if you truly need it or if it can be deleted later in the year.

❑ Declare email bankruptcy! - It's okay. Email bankruptcy is when you give up on ever getting your emails organized and decide to delete everything to immediately remove your email stress. You know you and the emails you receive best. So if this is your preferred action regarding your mess of emails, then do it. Delete everything and rest easy. Starting over may be your best option.

Habits, long-term goals, and the strength to complete them:
Why worry about habits when you're just trying to declutter your emails? You can't think of this as a one-time big cleanout. You've decluttered your emails. YAY! Sighs of relief. Clouds of confetti, parades, and balloons in celebration! But like any parade, there is the aftermath. Without following up with good decluttering habits, the digital dust bunnies will rapidly multiply again. Save yourself the stress of needing to complete this big decluttering process again!

❑ Form the habit - Timed declutter versus task-led declutter. It is important to distinguish between the two. A time-led decluttering is a specified amount of time taken each day or each week in which the goal is achieved. An example is the 15 minutes each morning and evening when I would whittle away at the massive backlog of emails I had. A task-led declutter is a specific goal of organizing 20 additional emails each day than what you received. Or 100 more.

Both methods will provide you with the ability to accomplish your goal, yet each speaks to a different personality type. Choose one or test each productivity option and keep going with the good habit you have started for yourself. These consistent habits of cleaning your email at least once per week will make all the difference in ensuring an organized digital life and avoiding a reversion to chaos.

PRO Tip: Keep track of your progress.
When you are keeping track of your progress with your digital life spreadsheet, I don't recommend marking your progress each day. Choose two specific days each week to mark your progress, such as a Wednesday and Sunday. Or one day a week is good, also. This is a bit like dieting; there are ups and downs and sometimes we are stuck at the same weight for a couple of weeks before we can make our way down towards our goal again. We all know there will be those days when a crisis of some kind will happen and our emails will suddenly be flooded, feeling like we've negated our progress for the week or month. That's okay. Life happens. When the crisis is over, file the ones you need to keep, delete the others, and keep going.

I discovered that the total number of emails doesn't show up in various apps such as Gmail, only the number of unread emails. Most of my work is done with my iPad Pro, so unless I power up my laptop, I'm not going to have stats for each email address every single day.

11 - Habits for the Long Term

While decluttering your digital life, what is to prevent it from becoming another mess to clean out in three months, a year, or five years? By developing good digital habits.

The daily deluge can be overwhelming, but it is manageable with a few personal rules in place. Knowing which emails are best filed, deleted, unsubscribed, and responded to will be a big help, but consistently staying on top of what enters our digital sphere will keep it contained.

This is a long-term process, a marathon, a full Ironman triathlon even. I thought it took about 21 days for a habit to form. I'm learning it's all a bit more complicated than that, but there are actions you can take to make good decluttering habits stick—many successful routines and habits to stay on top of your digital clutter.

Why is creating good decluttering habits so important?
A big declutter won't magically solve your problems of 17,000 emails and hitting your data limits in one area while maintaining 50 open GBs in another area. Creating good digital organization habits will help you keep your clutter in balance into the future.

How can you change the process or change your schedule to make it easier to jump into your next declutter session? When is it best to tackle the task?
How quickly does it all pile up? Will you need to spend an extra 15 minutes each day? What about weekly or monthly?

My favorite time of day to help maintain this habit is a short bit in the morning and then a short bit again in the evening, so no single task is too large.

❑ Start and end your day with good habits: AM Launch and Evening Setup - Each morning I have what I call an AM launch scheduled. I take a single, timed hour in the morning to catch up with overnight messages, emails, news, and social media. I use this time to get my digital life ready by doing such things as deleting anything that I don't need to move forward with and setting up my day to be productive. This builds the regular habit of digitally decluttering. Make the choice as to which actions you will take to launch your day. Yes, I've included social media here. The reality is that I'm going to visit a couple of my favorite social media sites anyway, so I might as well make it as efficient as possible.

❑ Create a click circuit - Your click circuit is your itinerary for your travels on the world wide web. I love my click circuit; mine is in a digital note with links so I stick to the itinerary and complete my circuit on the internet within the scheduled amount of time. Creating your own click circuit will help to keep your focus and reduce your mindless wandering through various social media and other websites.

My click circuit is a list of websites I frequently visit and how often I should check each of these accounts. Some of them are personal, wherein I need to connect with family members. Others are for business, and I need to check them daily, and sometimes even twice a day, to ensure the smooth running of my business.

You can create your own click circuit based on your starting line stats list. What do you need to check each day? Each week? Each month?

I find it much easier to work undistracted throughout my day after checking a few specific accounts, and having a quick list for me to refer to keeps me from venturing too deep down a random rabbit hole. You could set up reminders and notifications if that works better for your workflow.

So which accounts do I list?

❑ Feedly - This RSS feed brings my favorite websites to a single web page.

❑ Business selling accounts, including my website - Are they running well? Is all the information, sales, coupons, etc. up to date?

❑ Messaging accounts - I have friends all over the world, and it's great to read about their adventures and what they have accomplished in the time I've been sleeping.

❑ Class notes and messages - I do enjoy being a lifelong learner, and I need to check on homework and feedback from assignments.

❑ Evening setup - This is when I break things down, pack them up from my day, and get ready for the next day. I reset my home and digital life, so I prepare and set up things for the next day. I ensure the dishes are done, clothes are put away, and lunches are ready for the next day. How do you want to end each day? Think about how you want to start your digital day tomorrow. Think about how nice it will be to open an uncluttered desktop and have all the messy tabs from yesterday's research closed, with the files needed for the day's report together in a folder that is easy to find.

❑ Ensure all of your files are properly backed up - Do your evening setup at a reasonable time early in the evening such as right after supper. It's best for me to schedule this before I am too tired. It's okay to do additional work after your evening setup and then only have a couple of items to put away later on that night when you are ready for bed.

❑ Challenge: Set yourself a challenge to make tomorrow morning easier, such as deleting five more emails each evening session! Clutter accumulates daily, so building the habit of regularly decluttering will keep it at bay and keep your digital life a calm space to navigate quickly.

❏ Again, back up your work! - Breathe easier and sleep better tonight knowing that you are making progress towards a calm, digital life. In one year, by sticking to your small daily habits, you will reach your big goal of having an organized digital life. Any digital detox or vacations you choose to take will be just that, a true vacation away from your devices with minimal clutter upon your return.

❏ Pomodoro Technique - It's a productivity method created by Francesco Cirillo for effective time management. The popular task tool has you setting a timer for a short, specific period of time and to focus on that one single task until the timer goes off. It is usually set as a 25-minute period of time, followed by a 5-minute break, and then back into another Pomodoro period of time. It is based on the idea that we are most aware at the beginning and at the end of the work sessions. So if we keep work sessions just short enough to include this small set of attention span, we will be working at peak efficiency. This is sometimes called work sprints.

This is a great technique to help you get started on a task by offering you a simple 25-minute challenge, which then earns you a 5-minute break to keep your brain fresh. With these focused, short bursts of work, it is quite an efficient way to work, and when added together at the end of the day or the end of the week, the amount of accumulated work that is done can be astounding.

This can be adjusted for your own work needs. I use a 45-minute work and 15-minute break schedule, which works for my personality and work style. I start at the top of the hour and work for those 45 minutes, then take a 15-minute break to eat, stretch my legs, change over the laundry, or answer an email.

Then, at the top of the next hour, I am back at work, sometimes with the same task. Oftentimes, I am on to a new task that also needs to be done or moved forward today. And this is how I work through my day—a lot of task work, with a good amount of break time.

Find a timeframe that works for your tasks and personality. It's adaptable to your needs. A timer is easy to set up, is inexpensive, and is often already available on your smartphone.

Jump-start your decluttering with even a small five-minute sprint session. Doing a five-minute digital declutter followed by a 25-minute break to do non-screen time actions could work, too. It's about getting it done; it doesn't need to get done perfectly. I often have multiple projects going on at the same time, both personal and business, and they all need to move forward at the same time.

❑ Time blocking - This is a time-management technique to tackle time-based tasks as opposed to specific task-based to-do items. It is usually for a longer period of time so you can get into the flow of the task, with flow considered to be the optimal state of working in which you feel that time has flown by.

How to make digital decluttering a habit:

For long-term habit changes to become permanent, I had always heard it takes at least 21 days. But how accurate is this? Is it possible to circumvent this three-week timeline and form new habits faster? Or is the reality a much longer timeframe?

Turns out that the 21-day reference comes from Dr. Maxwell Maltz in the 1960s: ". . . commonly observed phenomena tend to show that it requires a minimum of about 21 days for an old mental image to dissolve and a new one to jell."

According to Gretchen Rubin when writing for The Happiness Project in Psychology Today:
> "It really takes 66 days. Yes, just over two months for many good habits to really stick. These 66-day numbers are from a study published in the European Journal of Social Psychology. The study also states that it can take up to eight

months depending upon the habit. Thankfully there isn't a super strict requirement that it absolutely needs to be 66 days straight."

Marking each habit task completed helps to reinforce the journey of successfully having an uncluttered digital life. Habit trackers are a strong part of many planner designs such as bullet journals. The act of marking shows accomplishments that may not be otherwise visible such as the consistent effort it takes to lose weight or learn a new instrument.

Habit trackers are effective because they feed into our need to keep the streak going and to not break the string of successes. Whether you track your habits in an app or on paper, it's the act of tracking that's important, the marking of an act completed successfully.

PRO Tip: Themed days of the week can break up the monotony of decluttering. Creating a theme for each day helps ensure you do a bit each day towards the large-scale decluttering project.
The themes I use are:
Money Monday
Talk Tuesday (for my smartphone)
Website Wednesday
Photo Friday.

Check-in: How is your progress?
❏ Write down your numbers - Keep track of each kind of progress, both the hard numbers and your time spent. Check in with yourself at the very least.

Digital decluttering is a long-term process, and along with good digital habits, it goes a long way to ensuring it is decluttered the first time and that it will stay that way. Understanding that there is a systematic solution to this extra stress is meaning you are winning the battle against digital clutter.

If your digital clutter is anything like mine was, this is an endurance event in three parts, much like a triathlon. Starting with the swim is your self-assessment, your starting line, and the first glimpses of your own digital minimalism. Bicycling is the second part where right-sizing, rearranging, and decluttering are your main goals. The final sport is the run, the marathon where you perfect your strides toward long-term maintenance through good digital habits.

Don't get discouraged if you have missed your "shoot for the stars" goal and lose sight of the fact you have still made a huge amount of progress already. Just like it takes a while to slow down and reverse a big snowball of debt, it also takes time to slow down and reverse the deluge of emails and documents that we work with daily.

It's okay to go away on vacation and suddenly find yourself with several hundred more photos to sort through. Set aside the time, write it in your schedule, and get right back on track to doing the sorting, and it will be alright.

PRO Tip: Rewards - What small thing can keep the momentum going for you on difficult days? Another mark in your habit tracker? Ten minutes of Candy Crush? Reward yourself and your family with gold stars on a chart or a new movie after decluttering the watch lists.

12 - Password Management

Your password system is a mess—just random bits of paper with mysterious scribbles in a pile on your desk or a haphazard mini notebook with random lists of more random notes. In the end, it's faster to create a new password than it is to search for the current one amongst the mess.

Maybe you've alphabetized that mini notebook and there is some semblance of order. But you really, really hope you never, ever lose it. Many of you have over 100 password accounts you are expected to remember, with a majority of them used at infrequent rates.

A listing of the most popular passwords used shows your exhaustion at password overload. You can't take the time to think of much more than birthdays, pets, and the dreaded "password."

In this day of required passwords, codes, and two-step verifications for everything from playing games to filing taxes, you are buried in letters, numbers, and symbols. You are begging to be relieved of this crazy mess of passwords. Time to change your messy, irresponsible password ways that you are living with now. It's time to learn an easy lesson on how to create stronger and more memorable passwords.

❑ One way is to have a good word you'll remember, such as

"Lemonade." Then add the site's name such as MyBank, with each word capitalized, and then a couple of special characters: LemonadeMyBank$@!

❏ Another way to create strong memorable passwords is to have a preferred sentence and add special characters.
"I drive my car to work every day" becomes IDMCTWED#!
Adding numbers creates stronger passwords: "Five days each week I drive my car to work" becomes 5DEWIDMCTW#!

❏ A third way to create strong passwords is to use a password storage option, such as 1Password, KeePass, or LastPass, in addition to the option on your own operating system.

There are additional companies that also provide these options. Research which company you feel most comfortable working with and has an interface you can understand.

PRO Tip: Want a quick way to answer those ridiculous security questions? Because, honestly, who knows when their great grandmother's favorite pet was born? Oftentimes the questions are creepy and way too personal. One way to put together consistent answers for various questions is to literally answer them all the exact same way, such as PetMyBank.

Or if it won't allow you to do that, take the noun of the sentence and add the company name, such as GrandmaMyStore, or use the verb or the last word in the sentence, such as BornMyStore.

PRO Tip: For security reasons, do not use an openly advertised email as your login emails.

After all of this, how many of you will now simply rewrite your slips of paper into a small alphabetized notebook that you can take with you in an emergency?

13 - Emergency!

Living on planet Earth is like choosing your own adventure in which disasters you feel you will survive. From hurricanes, earthquakes, tornadoes, flooding, and fire, you need to be prepared. When a disaster comes your way, you will need to have certain information available to make it through the sudden disaster happening in your life.

Copies of important documents can be stored in the cloud. Scanning apps such as Scannable, will make this easier. I'm very concerned about losing important documents and irreplaceable family photographs, so I save them in multiple places, enough places to let me sleep at night.

There is so much that needs to be ready to be prepared for an emergency, and your bug-out bag must be available for a quick grab and comfortable enough to carry a fair distance to an emergency shelter.

Being prepared for emergencies will increase your chances of survival and recovery more quickly. There are things you can do ahead of time to make your recovery a little easier.

Below is a list of items that can be backed up on the internet. Be sure to check websites such as American Red Cross or Fema.gov and specifically search for good, local information in your area about other items that need to be packed, from shoes to water.

Living in Japan, I need to be prepared for typhoons, floods, earthquakes, and fires at a minimum, and I need to plan for the fact that trains are unlikely to be running due to track damage.

What parts of your digital life need to be in our bug-out bag? What needs to be easily accessible in the cloud, and what should, if anything, be in paper form?

❏ Use your smartphone's health app to keep you and your family's health info for emergencies, including current medications and allergies. Some of the information that you need to enter can be accessed by emergency personnel if you are in an accident and unconscious. Yes, they can view it when they click "Emergency" on your lock screen without gaining access to your other phone information or apps.

❏ Update your contacts and ensure you add emergency contacts into your smartphone:
Doctors
Dentist
Partner's work numbers, and other coworkers' numbers
Children's teachers & principals, sports coaches, etc.
Poison control
Neighbors
Local emergency contacts

During a stressful emergency, it may be difficult to remember your partner's boss's name, so labeling it as Boss Beverly Jones will allow you to find and connect to them more quickly. Also, add a couple of secondary names and numbers from your partner's company, just in case Boss Jones happens to be away on vacation when you need to make that emergency call.

Add the following items to your digital bug-out bag and remember to generously use zip bags to keep items as clean and dry as possible.

❑ Backup external drives, USBs, and SD cards with important documents, such as driver's license, wedding certificate, apartment lease, mortgage info, medical records, tax paperwork, etc.
❑ Paper contact list in case your phone loses power, as you will still need the phone numbers to call from other calling options.
❑ Proof of insurance and the company's contact information—compile an accurate record of your possessions via photographs, serial numbers, and receipts. All of this can be stored digitally, so if you lose everything there is still a record of it. What's the best place for photos and information for the insurance company? Online? USB? I say both are best.

❑ Passwords

❑ Photograph of a check showing routing numbers for FEMA claims. To receive emergency funds from FEMA, you will need your bank account information.

❑ Extras - If you haven't already decluttered those extra cords, I recommend keeping at least one extra of each as needed for your emergency bug-out bag.

❑ Solar-powered or hand-crank chargers - Too often I've seen people have no time to get out of danger such as a fire, so even a fully prepared bug-out bag may be lost in the disaster. Ensuring your digital life is in order will help make your recovery after surviving a disaster easier for both you and your family.

❑ Döstädning or Swedish death cleaning - Originally referring to carefully, mindfully decluttering of your possessions before your death, including choices as to where your things will go after you have died. The same principles apply to your digital assets, your websites, and social media accounts.
❑ Choose how you want your accounts handled in the event of your death
❑ Choose who will have the passwords to your personal accounts and will follow through with your requests.

❑ Consider your business accounts as they can be extremely valuable to your partners and heirs to continue the good running of the business and the value of your estate.

Our lives are a dichotomy of strength and fragility, and planning for the worst while hoping for the best strengthens our resiliency. As another typhoon's heavy winds and rain batter my home, I feel stronger than ever that these emergency actions you need to take before trouble arrives are essential.

14 - Health: Body & Soul

It seems every aspect of our health care has been digitized. Even diagnoses are being made over video calls with medical professionals around the world. There are amazing feats in care, and then comes the confusing piles of medical billing. Ensuring you are connected electronically with your care providers and insurance companies is the best way to keep everything coordinated.

❑ Medical appointments and records - All of my medical communications, bills, Health Savings Accounts (HSAs), and insurance information is managed online in various portals. Each of these websites has its own passwords, and I then find I am automatically placed on their newsletter list. I wish that was illegal in the States as it is in other places. I worry that if I unsubscribe, I won't receive the billing information I need. So that is more email that I need to manage. I have literally received emails from my local clinic letting me know they have free coffee in the lobby on Tuesdays!

❑ Passwords - Managing my health means also managing a huge load of passwords and paperwork. Keep them safe.
❑ Paperwork - A lot of paperwork needs to be scanned, sent, and then digitally stored somewhere you'll never lose it.

PRO Tip: Health reminder regarding ergonomics - Ergonomics

is bioengineering that studies the connections workers have with their environment. I used to work at an office furniture dealership, and it's through these studies that you have great desk chairs to ensure you have good posture and the correct desk height to reduce injuries from sitting for long periods of time, including unique keyboards and keyboard trays to reduce carpal tunnel. In this chapter regarding health, consider the ergonomics of your relationships with your devices. Are you in a good sitting position with a good chair and desk, and are you able to keep your hands below your heart while typing?

❑ Fitness apps and equipment such as Fitbit, Garmin/Strava - From measuring .01 of a second in races to advanced medical devices giving freedom and options, computers have helped improve human capabilities in a myriad of ways. Using a Garmin sports watch pushes your race times ever faster in swimming, biking, and running. Power meters on racing bicycles, Fitbits for step counting, and weight-loss apps all have helped improve your health and fitness. While maintaining fitness for our bodies, these devices and apps need their own maintenance.

❑ Do the batteries need replacing?
❑ Is the charging station in a convenient place for your sports equipment?
❑ Are there connectivity issues? Are you having problems with the sports watch connecting with the heart rate monitor or uploading the information to the company's website for analysis?

Spiritual health - Nurturing your soul is as important as your physical health. Your computer devices are great tools with a variety of faith apps available at your fingertips. There are additional apps available to soothe your soul, from anxiety-reducing breathing exercises to Zen meditations.
❑ Delete as many of the poorly made, soul-sucking apps as possible.
❑ Search for the tools you need to keep the faith, heal yourself, and give your soul space to grow.

Your health is vital, so please take care of yourself and all of the digital connections you need to maintain your healthy lifestyle.

15 - Home, Pets, and the Internet of Things

Fully connected homes are no longer the vision of sci-fi writers and The Jetsons' cartoonists. The technology is here to stay and is making its way into more and more homes, including retrofitting older homes with their benefits. Even without the modern tech installed in your home, you likely have home and auto insurance, repair services, property taxes, and more that you maintain through internet websites.

Schedule the few minutes necessary to ensure you can access all of the accounts connected with the upkeep of your home. I have listed examples below; add the ones that are part of your household.
❑ Check that each of your accounts is still setup per the contract you signed on for.
❑ Ensure that your payments are being properly applied.
❑ Check for better options, such as new package deals and new offers.

Apply the above steps to any of the following accounts you own.
❑ Internet Provider - Your home is where your WI-FI internet connection comes in; have you checked on your internet provider's available plans recently? Check to see if there is a better plan at a better price for your internet needs.

- ❏ Mortgage/homeowners insurance
- ❏ Rent/renters insurance
- ❏ Auto insurance
- ❏ Boat, RV, etc. insurance

- ❏ Homeowner's association
- ❏ Neighborhood message boards

- ❏ Repair companies
- ❏ Lawn services
- ❏ Security - Services and cameras

Your peripherals, or items that are all part of the "Internet of Things" (IoT), loosely encompasses any products that have a way to electronically transmit data to or from the item out onto a network. That network could be either the internet at large or within a network in your own home such as using wireless earbuds over Bluetooth. These products you bring into your home are often labeled as "smart" items no matter how mundane the item is, like a "smart" toaster for example.

Not everything needs to be connected to a network just because it can. From privacy concerns to reduced product lifespans, make educated decisions regarding your own "smart" products. These items can include anything from your oven to your washing machine, your old digital camera to your lightbulbs to the video camera on your doorbell.

Go through your peripherals - We have more peripheral items supporting our digital life than at first glance. I've listed a few below for you to start checking. For me, this was a time to deal with all the little irritants around the house. Smart products are more and more ubiquitous, but they do not come without their own set of problems. It is time to see what's going on.

- ❏ Hook it up correctly so you can enjoy its full benefits.
- ❏ Leave it Luddite if possible; don't hook it up to a network and use it at its most basic.

- Pass it on, recycle it, or sell it.

Move through your home, room by room, starting with the entrance, to help you systematically check your peripheral IoT:

- House Systems: Amazon Echo, Google Assistant, etc.
- Security system
- Doorbell

- Refrigerator
- Oven - You can ask it to start preheating before you walk in the door to make dinner.
- Toaster

- Laundry - You can ask the washer to log how often you use the washer and to send an SMS five minutes before the washer is done. The dryer is considered a smart device also. You can ask to have specific music played when the cycle is done.

- Printer - Having trouble printing or scanning? Does it need new ink? A longer cord since it needed to be moved? Time to figure out your preferred configuration by hooking up the printer with a cord or setting it up for Bluetooth and email.

- Outdated peripherals - Are you losing peripherals to updates and they are aging out? Or is it time to do some sleuthing and find out how your otherwise still good, ten-year-old printer is suddenly not printing when all the ink cartridges are new?

- Old smartphone use - Consider setting up an old phone with the digital speaker as a permanent station to listen to your favorite podcasts in your home office or kitchen.

- TV remote - One day the Apple TV remote app works, and then the next day it doesn't. So back to the little sliver of a remote that gets lost in the couch cushions and is putzy futzy to search for specific items. Most of these do not necessarily fit into any specific "cleaning" category, but they need to be done for a smooth and comfortable running of your digital household.

Does your Apple TV app suddenly not work? Does the app need an update or does the Apple TV need the update? Or both? Or is the problem with the regular Apple TV remote? If it hasn't been lost in the couch cushions, does it simply need a new battery or to be recharged depending on the model you own?

As you move through your home, put together a list of these little irritants and start knocking them out one at a time. Get your family involved in helping; a task such as the TV remote app may be fixed by one of the older children in the family.

Not all of our peripherals are "smart" products; some are there to support the products and your devices, such as charging cords and data accessories.

❏ Charging station - Do you need to update your charging station? Clear out extra cords and the old cords that no longer can connect to any device you own. Do you need additional stations or to reduce the amount you usually have? Is the charging station in its most convenient place?

❏ Are the spare batteries fully charged? They need to be in a convenient place so you remember to keep them regularly charged for emergencies or to grab when you know you will have an extra-long day.

❏ Upgrade your cords as needed - Have your devices upgraded, and now you need a new SD-card reader with a USB-C option?

Pets - Yes, our pets. We have been asking them to join our digital lives, and they are indulging our overbearing entrance with our apps for cats and our video cameras that watch their every eating and drinking habit while we are away.

❏ Your pet's microchip - Our most beloved peripherals sometimes wander off on their own! Is your cat or dog chipped? Be sure all the information is up to date—phone number, address, current vet, etc.—which can all be accessed and updated through the chip company's website.

❑ Smart collars - Not only for location tracking, but also to monitor your pet's level of activity and to have two-way communication when they are out of sight.

❑ Edit your pet apps - How does your cat like the apps you downloaded? Were you entertained by your cat as much as your cat enjoyed the app? Rate it, keep it, or delete it.

❑ Food Bowl and water dish cameras - Remotely feed them while you are away, and watch them destroy the couch while you're at work. Pets are no end of entertainment for all of us, so keep your video cameras properly connected.

❑ Pet sitting or dog walking app - Do you need a professional pet sitter or dog walker? Or have you found these apps completely useless for you and your pet's needs? Add, update, or delete the apps as necessary.

Our connected homes, family, and pets can bring great benefits and necessary support for many of you, yet, leaving it Luddite can bring greater peace and quiet for others. Make smart choices for your smart home that fits you and your family best.

Check-in - Throughout the process, you should be doing periodic check-ins with yourself, with your decluttering quest partner, or with your team.
❑ Update your Digital Life List - Are you finding more digital accounts as you declutter? I remembered yet another email and IG account that I managed and added them to my digital life list. Add the new accounts you find to your starting line stats. Mark them off when you have decluttered them.
Are you sticking with the scheduled tracking of your weekly and monthly progress? This deep into the decluttering process will show you have made a huge amount of progress so far. Keep up the good work!

16 - Photos

When you consistently take the time to declutter your photos and videos, then by the time you're done, you'll have digital warehouse storage units right-sized and organized for your photography needs. That being said, your digital footprint has had years in which to grow, so it won't be reduced in a single day or even a week!

How many photos do you have that need decluttering on your smartphone alone? 2000? 8000? 14,000? 18,000? Maxing out the capacity of your phone slows it down a lot. In how many places and on how many devices are they scattered? In the cloud? On your external hard drives?

Update the photography section on your digital life list:
❑ on your devices
❑ in your device's cloud accounts such as iCloud, OneDrive, Google Drive, etc.
❑ professional storage sites such as Dropbox, SmugMug, Adobe Creative Cloud, Flickr, etc.
❑ photobook sites such as Shutterfly and Blurb
❑ camera, SD cards, USBs, CDs, etc.
❑ video

Referring back to your digital life list is vital to find out what assets you have, what space is still available, and where it is. This will help determine what you'll do with those thousands of photos: delete them, save them, or move them to another location.

❏ Declutter as a family - This is your opportunity to teach smart digital-organizing habits to the family members who are old enough to help. Set up files for specific family members, for different classes, for soccer season, for girl scouts, etc. Keeping the family informed will make everything go much, much smoother. They will also help keep you on track.

PRO Tip: Batch renaming of photographs by event or date is extremely helpful when organizing them. It helps when doing a quick search by a logical name such as soccer_2015.

❏ Group photos into smaller albums - The best way to tackle the thousands of photos you have is to break them down into smaller, more manageable groupings. Create folders or albums in which you separate either by date, event, place, or person. It's easier to find the best images when comparing camping photos with other camping photos, or when all the softball games are together. Break it down into files of each vacation day so you can feel the accomplishment in each baby step forward.

Edit a hobby or sport for each child; for example, one does football, one does karate, and the other takes art classes. Bring them into the choices for the photographs. You can group them together again into a single-year folder as a family for an end-of-year video.

❏ Captive decluttering task - Selecting photos for creating album subcategories is easily completed during captive decluttering sessions. Organizing, editing, and deleting the album from that camping trip you took with the family last summer during your captive decluttering time at the DMV is a worthwhile way to spend your screen time. You'll walk out knowing you've at least accomplished something!

❏ Start with the oldest photos first - The photos that bring us the greatest joy are usually the oldest, like the wonderful photos that remind us of how the rainforest smelled or the sounds of the elephant you fed. Photos like the ones taken during the summer at the beach when your child learned to swim are top memories to keep a few photos from, but you don't need to keep them all. Think of the highlight reel in your memories, and keep those as a guide through your photographs. Some photographs won't evoke the essence of the event. If there isn't a memory of what that photo is doing in your collection, then it's time to delete it.

❏ Delete your duplicates - Once you have isolated a group of photos, it's time to curate. There are programs to help you find the duplicate photos you have which are taking up extra data. Eliminating those at the beginning of your decluttering will give you a boost to start.

❏ Delete poor-quality photographs - Delete that blurry photo you accidentally took of the sidewalk. Delete the ones with your out-of-focus family members, the ones with your finger in the frame, or the video that is too shaky to see anything.

❏ Decluttering photographs with good habits - Use timed or task-based decluttering and a habit tracker. Staying in the habit of timed sessions to declutter your photos involves a reasonable set amount of time, such as ten minutes. A task-focused work session creates a goal such as decluttering 20 photographs in an evening.

PRO Tip: Schedule editing time, and don't wait! Pull yourself out of the "someday" habit. I had two photoshoots this week and am up to 4465 photos and 97 videos. Scheduling edits immediately when the shoot was complete has helped keep those numbers from being much higher!

❏ Long-term storage - Multiple backups are a good idea for your most treasured photos.

There are several sites for storing your photography, such as Flickr, Adobe Lightroom in the Creative Cloud, Google Photos, iCloud, Dropbox, etc. Some are created for photographers and have good features to support a photographer's needs for a lot of asset storage space.

By checking your digital life list, you know how much data space you have. Check out storage options and pricing and see if it's time to move things around to right-size your photo storage needs. You may find a less expensive and more user-friendly solution. Be careful regarding free storage cloud sites as free doesn't always stay free.

❏ Delete, delete, delete - Sending photos to the trash doesn't necessarily delete them forever. You are usually required to permanently delete the photos before you lose photos and gain back your GBs.

If you are unsure about permanently deleting a photo, don't worry. At this point, all your photos are usually sent to a "deleted" folder, which will keep your photos for an additional amount of time before they are permanently deleted, usually 30 days. Don't forget to take the extra step of permanently deleting if you are culling to find data storage space in your digital life. You will need to go directly to your "deleted" photos section and select for permanent deletion.

❏ Curate in waves - This is a process. Curate in waves until you reach your final goal. I find that I am unable to perfectly edit all of my photos in the first wave of deletions, nor the second, or even the third. Some images are in that gray area of yes. I'd like to delete them, but, what if . . .? So they sit in their photo folders, and in the next wave of edits, I may realize it's not that important or a similar one is better, and I can comfortably delete it.

PRO Tip: Sync phone and computer photos if the screen is too small for final editing. You may already have this with your operating system's cloud account. I know smartphone screens can be just too small to pick up important details you need to edit.

❏ Creating final products - Create final photography from slideshows to videos and photo books. Is there an upcoming anniversary, retirement, or birthday party? This is a great time to slowly start getting a fun slide show together. From fabric wall calendars to shower curtains, by using a company such as Shutterfly or Blurb to print out the book you compile in their easy-to-use program, you can then order multiple copies for extended family and friends.

Instead of a physical book, you can create slideshows or short videos with a combination of the photographs and videos taken of a ski vacation or a whole soccer season. The shows can still be stored in multiple digital locations to keep them safe, and it's easy to share with a large group of people, like a soccer team.

Plus, all those photos are also stored on the company's database. Double-check how long they will allow your photos to sit there, because after you have placed your orders, they have no requirement to keep your photos. So what about all those photos you've uploaded? You are encouraged to keep your created photos and saved photo books there with the thought you may want to order another copy in the future.

While a valid point, there is a limit. How long do you feel comfortable leaving your photos there? The photo book company has no obligation to keep your photos any longer than they want to, so I recommend keeping a copy of all photos you cherish in your own possession. Recently, I checked on my wedding photo book, which has been on Shutterfly for over ten years. I am able to reorder the book again if I'd like.

I feel comfortable deleting these from the website because I have all of those photos saved into other formats. I would also format the book differently, so I'm okay with the book design itself being lost.

❑ Check your peripheral photography apps - Do you still use all your photography-related apps, such as photo-editing apps, filter apps, watermark apps, and light meter apps? Keep the ones you use and delete the rest. If you are a heavy, long-time user of one of the apps, are there newer, better-functioning ones available?

For your progress, reward yourself and reward your family - This accumulation of photographs has taken years, decades, and literally a lifetime to your children. Each summer, I spent a couple of weeks with grandparents I lived far away from. My grandmother would save all her photographs for me to place into albums for her. It was a way for me to catch up with family I barely saw once a year.

Are the family photographs still in old-fashioned albums and need to be scanned? They will need to be merged into your folder system on your devices or possibly have them uploaded in the cloud for sharing.

Get your family involved, go over these great memories you have collected as a family, and put together a screen saver set, slideshow, or video for everyone to enjoy.

17 - Easing the Pain of Culling

All these deleting, curating, and culling techniques with our digital assets can be very painful. What if we delete something we need?

Reducing the pain of deleting too much:
❏ Taking out the trash - Deleting most things simply puts the items into a trash can. None of those items have yet made it out to the curb, into the dumpster, or onto the truck, nor are they buried in the landfill just yet. You can delete something and still have time to think about it. The trash on my laptop will sit there for years and years until I hit delete. This is depending upon your device and its operating system.

Some trash cans, such as the one for photos on my smartphone, are on a specific timer. My photos are set to automatically delete from this system in 30 days. So if I delete a photo, I have 30 days to fully recover it if I so desire. Otherwise, it will be automatically removed from my "deleted" folder.

❏ Create your own dumpster folder - Are you still nervous about deleting too much and can't even get it into the trash bin, just in case a family member accidentally empties it? Create a folder and call it what you want, such as "The Dumpster." Fill it up with all the items you'd like to delete permanently. Now set a date. Yes, set a date for when "The Dumpster" will be moved into your computer's real trash can for deletion.

If you do not set a date for deletion, you will let this file sit there like a big pile of smelly gym clothes, taking up data space. Set it for a week, a month, or even a year. See how it feels. You can see how much less cluttered your computer is, and you can feel a more comfortable workflow happening.

Does "The Dumpster" folder still make you nervous after your designated time is up? If you are not even thinking about it, that's great! Move it down to the trash bin.

If you are continuing to worry about something in that folder, if it's keeping you awake at night, that's a good indication there is a file just too important for you to let go. That's okay.

❏ Sweep everything into an archive file - Starting over is sometimes the best option. Starting over would feel better than this mess. Well, maybe that's what you need to do. Either by date or by subject, put it all together, whatever it is, zip it down as compact as possible, and put it into a storage unit. It doesn't matter whether it is in the cloud or external storage; either way, just pack it away like putting a book on a shelf. Your annual collection of files is like a yearbook. This is okay. This is about organizing your files in a way that makes sense for your life, resulting in the least amount of clutter to wade through on a day-to-day basis.

PRO Tip: Search files versus organized files - The fastest way to find well-named files is to use the search bar! There is a limit to how intensely we need to organize our clutter: we do not need to be obsessed with every single detail. Typing in search terms to find files is often faster than clicking through a file/folder tree for a specific file to open it even when you know where to search for the file. When you aren't sure which area to search, your digital clutter is a problem. When you are running out of data space, you need to be checking details and creating better digital-organizing habits.

This is not a perfect process. Too many files have gray areas, and too many photos have amazing memories attached to let them go easily. It's a process. What doesn't feel right to let go in the first wave may be right to let go in the second wave of culling—or in the third wave.

18 - Cloud Files

Files, files, files floating everywhere!
- ❏ Adobe Creative Cloud
- ❏ Dropbox
- ❏ Photography storage sites
- ❏ External storage devices
- ❏ Your operating system's cloud storage (e.g. iCloud, G-Suite)

Check-in with your digital life list and update the stats for each of your cloud accounts. Refer to these stats when deciding where to store your files. Consider what reallocation of files will make the most sense in relation to your workflow.

❏ Your most expensive cloud account - Start here, with your most expensive cloud warehouse units. Are you getting your money's worth? Do you need more?

❏ Your most congested cloud account - To move cloud files from one account to another, it is necessary to download them onto your computer. I like to use my desktop. My desktop is like my local train station for my files as they glide in and glide out like the bullet trains here in Japan. As you declutter your cloud accounts, keep your files moving smoothly through the station. Don't forget to delete the files from your desktop train platform at the end of the day.

❑ Create small groups of files together - This will create more manageable bites in which to rename. For example, files regarding a marketing proposal will be scattered between word documents, Evernote, and Photoshop, and once the presentation is completed, you can choose a more logical filing and naming system to make it easier to find the archived files.

❑ Renaming your files - How you consistently name your files is technically called file naming conventions.

A couple of file naming conventions to keep in mind:
❑ Choose a consistent date form: YYMMDD or MMDDYY or YYYY-MM-DD
❑ Capitalize each word to make it easier to read.
❑ If you need a space, use an underscore "_"
❑ Special characters aren't usually allowed.

Let's talk about naming all these files.
❑ Keep it simple and logical to you. Consider what is important about the files from the subject to the date and be sure they aren't too long.

Names that are too long become lost in the short space, making it difficult to see the full name. It makes it difficult to know which files I'm looking at without opening it up. Shorter names are a time saver for me.

Consider the project, the people, the event, the place, the class, the date, and its version when choosing your file names.

How deep should I organize my files? In other words, how far should I go with files inside of files to be the most efficient with my digital decluttering? The fastest way to find well-named files is to use the search bar!

Some projects will require more than others, but the real test is how quickly you want to access your files. Click after click after click to reach just the right one can be really annoying. Using tags and a good file name is even better.

19 - Perseverance: The Long-term Project

Digital decluttering is a long-term project. You did not accumulate this mess overnight. It will take time to slow the accumulation and reverse course. You can cram all the decluttering into a much shorter period of time if you'd like, but please be careful of the stress that too much screen time places on your body. We'll start with the big picture and drill down into more and more details as you progress.

Long-term projects have their ups and downs, and there are identifiable stages for successful long-term projects:

❏ "Why am I doing this big decluttering project?" You know you need to declutter, but really? Today? It's a gorgeous day out! You love the outdoors and you've suffered through another chilly winter. Time to look ahead and focus on your end goal. Ask yourself what it will feel like when it is decluttered and you can easily move between files and programs you use on a daily basis. Your earning potential will increase the more organized you are, and you will be more ready for personal and work changes.

❏ Big long-term projects begin to take on a life of their own -

Oftentimes projects that take this long can become monsters all on their own. Digital decluttering is a huge task. It's annoying, it's boring, it's a mind-numbing evil monster that must be slain. It's more difficult than we originally anticipated. The day-to-day slog through the steamy swamp of our digital declutter isn't pleasant.

This is when you need to break your progress down into even smaller steps. Is your personal challenge of 20 more emails than you receive each day greater than you can handle on sunny summer days? An updated challenge could be five more on sunny days but 25 more on rainy days. It may slow your progress, but progress is progress. The tortoise beat the hare. Take the win; you're still making progress. You can also look at *The BIG Checklist* and choose another task. But then you have a whole other bit of psychology at work there: procrastination.

❏ You are at your low point, thinking it's not worth the extra stress and all this extra screen time. You don't want to be on the quest for a clean and dreamy digital life anymore so you're ready to quit. This is the time to change your approach and your thoughts regarding your decluttering project. This is a process and you can change your mind. Take a look at the process itself, the simple act of making room for better photos and videos in the future. The process is the act of taking care of an expensive device and all of the accounts that go along with it. Proper maintenance and care go a long way in the life of your computer. All of my decluttering has helped me learn a lot about my devices and their operating systems.

❏ Keep strong connections with your check-in partners and accountability team. A strong support network can be the difference between your success with digitally decluttering or not. Support each other and be accountable.

❏ Share your digital stats - Share your successes. Choose specific days and times to show your progress—every Thursday and Sunday at 9 PM, for example. Show your work. Regularly post your progress. Show your line graph, your gold star stickers, or your marked habit tracker.

❑ Show your failures - It's okay if the numbers go up for a while. Jump back in as soon as you can and start moving those email numbers down again. Start organizing more photos into slideshows. Consistently keep yourself and your partners accountable.

PRO Tip: Take regular breaks. Have you been taking at least one day off of the challenge per week? Digital decluttering is a daunting task, often mind-numbing and sometimes even painful. Constant hours and hours staring at the screen brings on headaches and backaches. We already have too much screen time, and this digital declutter project could be adding to your overloaded screen time.

Screen health, eye strain, and headaches - Do you find you are getting headaches more and more frequently, especially after long days of computer and smartphone use? Definitely take steps to limit your screen time and get your eyes checked. There are several actions you can do to reduce eye strain so you can get back to decluttering after your eyes have properly rested.

❑ Limit your screen time - Too much screen time is unhealthy and part of the reason complete digital decluttering of your life takes such a long time. Too much extra screen time will make it impossible to complete any work at all.
❑ Adjust the brightness level of your screen.
❑ Turn on the dark-mode option, if your screen is still too bright.
❑ Night Mode - I use the night-mode setting during the daytime also unless I'm out in the bright sunlight. Night mode reduces the blue light coming from your smartphone and tablet.
❑ Accessibility Options—Larger font size and larger icon sizes reduce eye strain when trying to read on smaller smartphone screens.
❑ Glasses—Get the best glasses possible if you need them. Your eye strain may be caused by simply aging, and inexpensive readers will be helpful when reading smaller smartphone screens. You may or may not need blue light blockers. I chose not to get them as they change the color of what you are seeing. For me as an artist who agonizes over color choices in my practice, they are not a good choice.

❑ Digital declutter in waves—Keep peeling away the layers of clutter, account by account, file by file. When scraping away at the clutter, I hope you will see why you brought the device into your life in the first place. Rediscover apps that make your life easier. The first waves scrape away the largest amounts of clutter initially, but it is the additional waves when going through all of our clutter that we make the most meaningful changes.

You'll go back through your files, folders, and accounts, moving more and more layers of clutter, yet again, and see you don't really need more of those files, or a fewer number of your photos are as precious as you initially thought.

Be persistent; you'll begin to see an end in sight. The files will be smaller, the maxed-out data notices will be fewer and soon disappear, and you'll get in the groove of the process.

Look how much you have decluttered thus far. You have the knowledge you've gained and *The BIG Checklist* to keep going and see this through to the end. See what you have already completed:

❏ You've cleared off your desktop - The first glimmers of the power you had to take command of your digital life was by clearing off your desktop. To have your laptop start up with a great wallpaper of your own choosing with no clutter feels great! Your train station platform runs smoothly.

❏ You've optimized your desktop dock - Having your favorite apps lined up just right in the dock, ready for you just as you need is about you choosing the most efficient way for you to move through your digital life.

You're making headway with your emails, you're right-sizing your digital storage, and the bumps in your workflow are smoothing out. Remember, this is a marathon project.

Always mark your wins. It doesn't need to be big, and it doesn't need to be money spent on a physical reward. Sometimes simply marking your spreadsheet showing your progress is enough.

Celebrate your wins!

20 - Smartphone

Decluttering your phones can be both your easiest task and your most difficult. Your smartphone is with you always, but it also causes you the most distractions with their repeated notifications from various friends, family, social media sites, and emails.

It is in your phones where you can grab the smallest bits of time to make the greatest progress. Keep up with the captive decluttering by using the minutes you have while waiting at the dentist's office or in line at the bank. If you take public transportation, you have these additional hours each week to ensure your phone and even your tablet is the most up to date.

Your phones are where you take your photos and record much of your video. Part of the captive decluttering you can do is sort through those photos. We are always taking more and more photos as we move through our days. Some of us have thousands of photos just sitting in the photo app that need decluttering. When I get home, I declutter in these smaller, bite-sized pieces on my phone, then do the final edits and deletes on my tablet or laptop where I can see them all much easier.

❑ Network provider - Do you need to make changes? Can you save money by moving to a different company or a different package? Do you need to find one with better reception? Are you happy with which credit card or prepay option you are currently using? Block out the time to take care of this! Check if you can make the changes via their website, which will cut down on the time required to make changes.

❑ System Preferences app - This is similar to the process covered in Chapter 7. Your utilities app is the control center of your phone. Going through each section in order will show you a multitude of options available to make the most of your smartphone experience.

❑ Fully update your smartphone - Update all the apps too.

❑ Accessibility settings - These settings really help improve your smartphone experience. Can you see everything on the screen or are you squinting a lot? Should you make the font show larger?

❑ Audit permissions, notifications, and privacy

❑ Turn off PUSH notifications

❑ Manner mode/vibrate - My favorite decluttering action with my phone has been to turn off all notifications. Yes, all of them. Turn the phone onto "manner mode" so it doesn't ring in restaurants or other places that would be impolite. At home, I can easily hear the buzz of the vibrate mode. There is no longer the need to check every single note that comes out of that device. Give yourself a rest.

❑ Dock apps - Move your most important apps here. I have my Kindle app, favorite messaging app, email app, and note-taking app here. Move the phone app from the dock to another screen. I have long since moved my phone app away from the dock and the home screen. I simply never use it. It still works the same no matter where it is on your phone.

❑ Language keyboards - Are all of your language keyboards up and running, and the dictionary apps to go with them?

❑ Business versus personal - If you have separate phones, are you properly connected on your business phone? Do you need to delete an app on your personal phone that should only be on your business phone? Enforce your vital work/life balance by removing it from your personal phone.

❑ Check your emergency numbers and info - This is so important that I'm listing it a second time. Completing the emergency medical information in your smartphone's health app will allow emergency medical personnel a way to access your emergency contact and other vital information you provide.

How can they access it on my locked phone? The 'Emergency' on your locked screen does more than call emergency services; it also provides access to this specific section of vital information you need to type into your health app.

Keeping your contact list updated and as clean as possible will make it easier in an emergency for your family to find who they need to connect with. Sure, they may have your boss's number to call in an emergency, but do they have the number of someone else when the boss is away on vacation and you can't come into work because of a medical emergency?

❑ Update or delete old contact information - I noticed I had a locksmith's number from three moves ago back in another country. That's just contact number clutter. I have many friends that move as often as I do, so having old info for a friend who has moved twice isn't helpful.

Time to cull the phone list so it is easier to find who you are interested in connecting with. Who do you have in your list of contacts that doesn't need to be there? Have some of your family members moved and have a new phone number, but you still have their old numbers? Do you still have numbers of old real estate agents or a great plumber from four moves ago?

Add your current friends . . . while you may connect easily through a social media app right now, what happens in an emergency? It's best to have multiple ways to connect to keep your connections strong.

❏ Organize the apps - Get rid of your excess apps using the provided option within your operating system. iPhones have a feature where it deletes, or at least hides, the ones you don't use. I hide the rejects I can't delete on the last page in the following screens by subject.

I prefer to curate my most used apps on the first page, and then the rest are placed in folders. Any remaining apps you have after deleting your unused ones can be consolidated into folders and given a category name to easily find them later. Of course, in recent updates from Apple, it's possible to do more efficient sorting of apps, bringing it alongside other features in your smartphone. Until I update my tech, this saves time from flipping through a lot of pages searching for the app I want to use.

❏ Deleting Apps - Delete as much information as possible within the app before deleting the app if you are doing so permanently. I have encountered an app or two that have not kept up with the times and stopped working beyond specific updates on my smartphones. Be aware of the apps that are not making updates, as they may soon not work any longer or be a security risk. Deleting an app to temporarily save on data space or because you want to clean things up does not mean your account with that app company goes away. You can delete your Spotify app but your account with Spotify isn't deleted. It's still there with the company. So don't worry about deleting most apps from your smartphone. Reload the app when you need it again and have the data space, and the account should be there.

Organize your apps as it suits your needs:
❏ Most accessed in the front, followed by those only occasionally used.
❏ Organize apps by category - all of my social media apps are on a single page.
❏ Put your business apps together - Adobe apps are on a single page.
❏ Organize them by folders and strategically place those folders

throughout the pages with the apps you need to use on the front page and the social media on the back pages.
❏ Organize your apps by color. Alternatively, change them all to black and white.
❏ Simplify your home screen - Create wallpaper that is a single soothing color such as all white or all gray and keep all apps off of the opening home page.

❏ Photo Organizing - My phone is usually my first step when it comes to photo editing and decluttering. I like to place photos into smaller albums to create more manageable-sized numbers of photos to reach my goal of edited and organized photos. My smartphone screen is too small to make final edits on the photos comfortably, but I can at least organize them into albums by event or date so they are ready to go when I get home to a computer with a larger screen.

PRO Tip: Save space on your phone - Some apps allow your phone to automatically back up to various cloud options. From an iPhone, you can do automatic backups to Google Photos for free up to 15GB, therefore opening up space in your iCloud for other digital assets. After that is done, you can delete the photos from your phone. Be aware that free cloud storage often moves into pay cloud storage at a later date. Things are rarely free forever, as a photography friend of mine has learned the hard way.

❏ Update your wallpaper - Don't forget to have fun where you can. Did you take a photo you would like to have as your smartphone wallpaper? Use it and enjoy it!

❏ Voicemail and old messages - Update your voicemail message if you need to and delete old messages. Over time, the photos and videos sent to you by friends and coworkers add up to quite a bit of storage space. Your data storage can be seen in the utilities or systems section, and you'll see if you need to make deletions in this area.

❏ Podcast apps - I enjoy listening to podcasts, but since I have had such a hard time with the podcast apps, I am going to just stream them from now on until I need to download a few episodes for when I'm traveling.

❑ Close your open tabs - Add this to your evening set up. Do you really need that many tabs open? If you haven't checked on it in the last couple of days, you probably don't need it. Save the link and file it away in a note. Now close down all those tabs and start fresh in the morning. Your app will run a little faster for it.

❑ Your online phone number - Using an online phone number that is available through companies such as Google Voice or Skype is very convenient for those who live and work internationally and want to maintain easy and consistent contact with family members and businesses. Family can call the number locally and can reach you wherever you have an internet connection. Your business customers will have a single number where they can also reach you. Oftentimes a different country means a different mobile network, so it's best to change your SIM card or you'll be hit with extremely high roaming charges. You can obtain an online phone number at a reasonable cost with services such as emailing when someone leaves a voicemail message. It is especially convenient for my family members who still prefer to communicate via phone without incurring international charges on their phone bill. You're welcome, Mom!

This is a big list to organize your smallest of devices. Your smartphone is small but it is your most powerful device because it is always conveniently with you, yet inconveniently, it leads to your biggest time-wasting. You now have better ideas to help make it a stronger device to help you grow, help you relax, and help you stay connected with those who are the most important in your life.

21 - Website

I have yet to meet anyone who is happy with their website. It's an organic creature that grows and morphs like an amoeba in ways you ask it, and you wish it was a better reflection of yourself or your business. As you change and grow, so should your website.

I make this a weekly action with "Website Wednesdays." If you complete one task per week, that's over 50 items each year. Time to start decluttering your website!

❏ Domain - Pay attention to your domain name! If your whole business brand is centered around your domain name, make sure everything is in order. Is your credit card information up to date on the domain company's website? Are you happy with your domain company? You often will sign up for a three- or five-year plan and then forget about it. If your credit card is not current, you could lose the name when you need to renew your domain! You have worked too hard to lose it. Mark your calendar for one month before renewal to iron out any bugs in the process before the renewal date arrives.

❏ Backup your website! Yes, the whole thing. Back it up. Back up your website regularly, just in case. How would you feel if you accidentally and irreparably lost your website? Yes, back it up! A site like WordPress has several plug-in options to make this process as easy as possible. Download one of your preferred backup plug-ins and complete the process.

We'll wait.

It's that important.
.
.
.

❑ Update your website software - Time to check if your website software is up to date. Are you utilizing your website to its fullest? Is the free level all you need? Do you need a greater level of software and service? Do you no longer need premium services and can reduce costs by choosing a different plan? Watch for sales on the various website plans in the email you send your miscellaneous junk emails from companies. You may find big savings.

❑ Security - Paid, full-service sites, such as the business option at WordPress, or even the free but limited blogging sites often have their own security, so there isn't a lot you can do to improve it from the user end except having a strong password. You've backed up your website, correct?

❑ Strong login passwords - Choose strong passwords that you'll remember.

❑ Limit login - Limit the number of times somebody can attempt to login to your website by using a limit login plug-in and keep it up to date.

❑ SSL (Secure Socket Layer) - Your website will be ranked lower in searches if your SSL is not up to date. This is available through your domain or a full-service site such as SquareSpace.

❑ Plug-ins - Are they all up to date? Be sure you have the latest version available. Periodically check when the program itself was last updated. If it's been over six months, check into other, newer plug-ins that do the same thing. It may be that the developer has abandoned that program and it is now vulnerable to security breaches.

❏ 404 errors - Check for broken links on your website. Each time I create a blog post, there are several links I add for my readers to find additional information. Sometimes it's source materials, sometimes it's products, sometimes it's the location of an event I recommend, and if that link is broken, I've sent my readers down a dead end. They are stuck staring at a 404 error! I don't appreciate it when it happens to me, so I make every effort to catch these errors as soon as possible.

WordPress has a great plug-in that checks for bad links within your site and on your blog. If you've referenced a company, an artist, or a magazine article that has since been deleted or changed, this plug-in will give you an itemized list of all the links that are no longer functioning. This can be a lifesaver if you have years of blog posts you would otherwise need to check by hand.

❏ Curate your blog posts - I usually curate my blog posts along with running plug-in to check for broken links. This is a good time to update or delete old posts that may have become irrelevant. Sometimes the blog post was in support of a one-time event that no longer adds to the complete message or theme of your blog.

Depending upon the subject and frequency of your blogs and websites, you may need to do this as often as once per month. Usually, I do this every six months. If you are running out of space, be sure you still want each of your blog posts.

❏ Answer customer comments - Connecting with your customer base is vital, so you need to stay on top of incoming messages and properly respond as soon as possible. Delete any spam messages that leaked through the filter.

❏ Update your theme - This is necessary for both security reasons and to keep your site looking fresh. Are you happy with the theme of your website? Happy with the color? What would you like to update with the look of your website?

Have fun with this as much as you can, but definitely back up your entire blog first in case it doesn't work as planned. Then you can do a quick reset and bring the older version back online with minimal disruption to you and your clients.

Let your customers know you've updated your theme. It's a good conversation starter, and it is good to warn your customers who are more security conscious.

Doing the updates when they become available usually opens up fun new features to implement on your website! Read exactly what is being updated and make changes to your website accordingly.

❑ Profile and your logo - Are your identifying photographs and logo well done? What about the photos you are using for your banner photo, your profile photo, or your logo? Great photographs make a huge difference in your professional presentation.

❑ Newsletter - Newsletter services are provided by companies such as Constant Contact or Mailchimp. Ensure they are properly connected with your website in the way you feel will be best for your customers. How do you want your pop-up to look, when should your customer see your pop-up, or do you prefer the embedded sign-up option? Test it! I love the digital newsletters that you can put together and let your clients know about what you've been doing and where you are going. There is a steep learning curve to get the adjustments and your consistent message done well, but it's worth it.

❑ RSS feed (Real Simple Syndication) - Ensure your website is set up for RSS so your clients and fans can read your latest postings comfortably on a reader app such as Feedly. Give your readers and customers every opportunity to connect with your brand.

❑ Shop settings - If you sell on the internet, check all of your shop settings. Is your shop page up to date? Your customers have a lot of clicks they need to do to complete the purchase of your products. Check that each of the steps along the way work as they should. Is there a supporting app for your shop, such as Etsy seller or WooCommerce, that needs to be downloaded? Do so and check the settings to ensure you can quickly respond to your customer's questions and concerns.

❑ Remove old announcements and update sales - Set an alarm to remind yourself when your sale ends on the website. It looks really unprofessional on a website when it says the sale ends on a date that was three weeks or even three months ago! Same with event announcements.

❑ Analytics - Set it up and check them. Do you need to update your site when your blog posts go out? Should you change the Search Engine Optimization (SEO) in the posts to get more traction?

❑ SEO and Keywords - Set them up, write them in, and check your analytics to help improve your reach.

Keep this list nearby for your "Website Wednesday" task list to improve your website. Completing one task each week is over 50 maintenance and improvement website tasks completed in a year!

22 - Social Media

In between a move or two, I lost the password to one of my favorite messaging accounts. I didn't lose much for digital assets, but I lost one way to connect with long-time friends. Moving from Japan back to the States meant I needed a new smartphone as Japan has a locked mobile phone system.

Therefore, it was impossible to recover the account because I had no way to receive a two-factor authentication code through the Japanese smartphone. Instead, I simply made a new account and luckily was able to reconnect with my old friends again after sending them an email letting them know what happened.

Two years later when I was back living in Japan, I reactivated the old smartphone. My old LINE account was there, working as though I'd never been away, welcoming me to my old clutter and confusing my friends as they now weren't sure which account to use.

Just like that, I had new clutter I had to deal with. I needed to decide which account to keep, which made me take a second look at all of my social media accounts and ask myself, "What is the purpose of these accounts?"

The easiest way to begin is to distinguish between personal and business accounts and make your decision from there.

❑ Check your digital life list - Update it with your current accounts. In this chapter you'll curate and delete your accounts.

❑ Account profiles - Go through each of the profiles and account information to see if that is how best to present yourself or your company moving forward. Are they on-brand for you? Do they have the right profile photos, the correct blurb, and the correct contact information to your website?

As you compile your digital life, you'll begin to see several accounts that you had forgotten about, some you visit less frequently but still like to connect with, and still others you visit more than you probably should. I no longer use my Tumblr account, but I do keep it updated as a billboard on the digital highway towards my most up-to-date endeavors.

You have grown as a person since starting several of those accounts. You probably no longer like the profile image, or maybe your location has changed and you no longer are posting from college but are on your third management promotion yet your profile says otherwise. Or maybe you have updated your avatar and should have a new image to reflect your personal growth.

Do you need all new professional images for your business accounts? Or do you have a few good images in your files? Some accounts will allow you to update your username—have you grown beyond that one you used when you thought you'd be a snowboard world champion, especially since you instead chose the occupation of a mechanical engineer?

Do you want your profile to show your accomplishments as a tri-athlete or reflect your prize-winning book illustrations?

Do you need to update your location? Some accounts such as Meetup will help you connect with other niche groups such as the local dog-owning chess players club.

❑ Too much information - Have you provided too much information, not realizing the internet wasn't as private as you thought? Check each of your social media accounts on your digital life list and make more educated decisions regarding how you want to present your digital life in relation to your life in the real world.

PRO Tip: I recommend keeping personal and professional social media accounts separate. Keeping a separate social media account for your business allows you to keep all communications very on-brand for the long term. Your personal life will go through a lot of changes and ups and downs over the years, which is normal, with your family and friends there to be supportive through thick and thin. Professional clients have their own ups and downs and want the security that through it all they can count on your work being solid. Don't hide your vacation days and sick days; keep them professional and on-brand. Honesty is important!

How do you want to move forward with your various social media accounts?
❑ Edit?
❑ Delete?
❑ Be a more focused, active user?

Personal User:
❑ Bio or "About Me" - There is nothing like one's favorite books or music to give insight into someone's personality. Add several of your favorites, and make connections with others that love the same.

❑ Who to follow/unfollow - Are you following the best accounts for your soul? Do they lift your spirits? Remind yourself what is most important. Are they respectful to you and your other followers? Do they make you think and help you grow?

❑ Decluttering socials - Do all of your social media apps need to be on your phone? Of course not. Pick just one or two that is the highest priority for you. It may be the one that is a messaging app that is used by the family, your car club, or the neighborhood baseball team. Only keep the ones that are most essential for you and delete the rest or move them to the back page on your smartphone.

❏ Family communication - Is there a single app and group where both local and distant families come together to chat and be on the same page? Time to update the family group chat if the current app isn't working for you.

There are a lot of group chat options to choose from such as LINE, Skype, Zoom, etc. There is no need to be faithful to any specific app that is causing difficulties in family communications.

❏ Turn off notifications - I mentioned turning off your notifications in the previous chapter on smartphones and it still applies to your other devices with regards to your social media accounts. Are you sure you need to receive a noisy, distracting notification from your social media apps? Having a balanced social media life can be very difficult. The algorithms are based on gambling tricks to keep you hooked, yet you need to be social to connect with clients and keep those same clients happy. It helps me to turn off all notifications on my social media apps so it doesn't pull me in when I have other appointments on my schedule.

PRO Tip: Always keep your professional social media sites up to date, such as LinkedIn and other industry sites. You never know when the next opportunity will come along or when the company you work for suddenly restructures. Keeping connected with others can help you see other opportunities for yourself and make a smooth transition into a new workplace.

❏ Publishing blog posts - Whenever you create a new blog post, is it set up to also send out to your preferred socials when you publish? If so, is it going to the best social media accounts possible, in advantageous formatting? Double-check all these connections and how they appear. Updates are always being made, and if you are not getting what you like, such as the photo showing on Twitter as you'd like or not, then you need to make your own updates.

❏ Update as new socials come out - Are you utilizing new socials?

Make the changes with your blog postings. Same for your professional product postings. Are they connected so everyone knows when your latest designs are with your satisfied clients?

❏ Are you ready to move from personal to business social media? Are you creating all new accounts? Do you need to create a business account in addition to the personal one you already have?

❏ Business accounts - Etsy, Shopify, and Not On The High Street are important avenues for many businesses and are sometimes a business's only website. Treat these as professionally as if it was your own website. It is through these websites that you can still connect with your clients with your social media accounts.

❏ Link to your shop - Be sure your socials are set up to direct your clients to your shops for them to easily make purchases. All of these apps work in tandem to help build successful businesses. Keep them open, and remember, it is called social media for a reason. Be social =)

❏ Website - Set up your social media streams to show within your website. Are each of your professional social media accounts connected with your website so your clients can reach you through their preferred channel? You want to make it easy for current and potential clients to connect and follow.

❏ Connect to your newsletter - Informing your clients, both current and potential, about your newsletter through your social media accounts is a good idea. If you want them to sign up for your newsletter, be sure to include the link to go directly to the newsletter sign up. Don't send them to the home page on your website and expect them to search through your site for it. Potential clients will give up if it's too much work and takes too much time.

The best thing about social media connecting is that you do not have to do any of it if you don't want to. There are still conventional pathways to success. You can communicate with some of your clients by word of mouth, an email newsletter, or in-person events, and you can give your fans lots of opportunities for them to spread the word about you and your work. Your connections to your friends and clients are up to you. Take command of your digital life by asking others to support your work.

❑ Posting socials - Do you have Hootsuite or Later for scheduled posting? Each of these are for you as a consumer of social media and also as a content creator of social media, such as Pinterest, etc. Do you have everything set up for you to easily post for your business? Take a look at these options. If you use them, a lot of the social media pressures will drop away. Planning for various commercial events is really important, and having another bit of support has been great. You need to let your clients know what you have to offer, and you know they like to see some of the processes while you are creating. There are great little apps out there that even a quick ten-second video can make a really great difference such as Spark Post and Adobe Rush.

❑ Advertising - Check your ads, the analytics, and the money for advertising on IG, Twitter, or FB.

❑ Money - You have a plethora of social media apps in which to support others and earn from others to move your lives forward, such as Patreon, Kickstarter, GoFundMe, and Twitch. Are yours set up how you want? Do you need to update information such as your banking accounts? Have you been considering opening up an account? Take a deeper look today at the pros and cons of it. Start a notebook in your favorite note-taking app to compile the tasks you need to do to open your own Patreon or Twitch Channel.

PRO Tip: Social media parking spaces - As a business, it is difficult to keep up with all the different avenues, highways, and fickle nature of the internet. When a new app comes out, we don't know if that's another bandwagon we should jump on or just stick with our tried and true apps.

As a business, a brand name is extremely important, so I have taken the path of "jump in and grab my parking space," if you will. I set up an account with my business name, essentially ensuring I can use that name and no one else can coincidentally use my name in a way that is divergent from my brand. I consider these accounts as billboards on the information highway. I provide information as to where I can be found, or an image or logo for someone to find me on another platform. Sometimes I have gone back and found a great way to use that platform, and other times, I just periodically update the "billboard."

❑ Unfollow - You're following a lot of accounts and it's cluttering your feed. Unfollow those whose content does not contribute to you positively. Whether it is entertaining or informative, be sure it is interesting for you.

❑ Twitter - Are those you are following still posting? Are you still interested in the subject in which they are posting? And how did you end up following a "Win a Mansion" account that last posted in 2009? That's a delete for sure! It is irrelevant as to whether they follow you or not. If it is clogging your feed and, as a result, taking up your time, unfollow! Check your bookmarked tweets; do you still need them? Have you forgotten about a good informative one?

❑ Instagram - I love the little "Save Later" on Instagram a little too much, so when I suddenly have over 500 saved posts, that's a huge pile of items, most of which I don't need anymore. I wouldn't be able to find something I saved if I wanted to. Time to "Unsave" and start over.

❑ YouTube - Check your "Watch Later" list on YouTube. How long is it? How many hours of video do you have sitting there? And just how old will you be when you finally get through all of it if you add no more videos to the list? Some of those videos will no longer exist by the time you get around to watching them.

❑ Pinterest - Go through your Pinterest boards and cull content that is old or that detracts from your brand. Delete boards that are no longer used. Make your decisions regarding your board's secrecy. Some are there to stay, and some are ready to be shown.

PRO Tip: Sanity and Safety - Many accounts now allow you to remove someone from following you without informing them. Other

options include the ability to separate yourself from that person or account digitally.
- ❑ Mute
- ❑ Block
- ❑ Hide
- ❑ Unfriend
- ❑ Unfollow

Take command of your social media accounts whether they are personal or business accounts. Have a purpose with each account and curate its content in keeping with that purpose. Be social on your social accounts and remember your options when certain followers are no longer respectful.

❑ Check-in: Keep marking your progress - Time to check-in on how you are doing so far with eliminating your huge pile of emails. Are you keeping track of your progress on your digital life list? Are you marking your streaks in your habit tracker? What is your longest streak so far? Do you need to make adjustments to your habit tracking goal to a more reasonable amount? Also, consider if you should be taking breaks at least one day each week to rest away from a screen. Be sure to celebrate milestones along the way to your bigger goals!

23 - Your Digital Money Life

Every photo that takes up data space in an account you pay for pulls at your wallet. That money comes out almost invisibly, automatically charged to other electronic accounts. Each one is usually a small, seemingly insignificant amount, such as $0.99 here, $5.00 there, or even $50 for some programs. These monthly deductions add up quickly and are like a digital hole in your pocket!

How would we make our money decisions if we needed to write a check for every small digital transaction, put it in an envelope, stick a stamp on it, and mail it at the post office?

I have found it a very effective habit to group tasks together. By creating a block of admin accounting time every Monday called "Money Mondays," I have created the habit of working on at least one new task each Monday. That comes out to 52 actions each year. This has ensured I take a critical eye to repair any digital hole in my pocket. Your finances are too important to ignore, and good financial habits will help make your dreams come true.

Banking:
Start your financial digital declutter quest with your bank accounts. They are central to your financial picture to receive your income,

obtain cash from an ATM, and use your credit cards.

❑ Digitally accessing your bank accounts - Can you properly access your bank accounts and initiate account transfers? Reduce real-life clutter by turning off paper statements.

❑ How do you prefer to access your bank accounts? Do you want to use the app on your smartphone? You can load the app when you need to use it and then immediately delete it when you have completed the transaction. For security reasons, I don't feel comfortable having my banking apps on devices that can so easily be lost or stolen.

❑ Do your banking accounts have your correct address and phone number since moving?

❑ Have you had a problem with your checking account and needed to get a new account number? Needing to change your accounts can have a cascading effect on any of your bills and other accounts. I encountered a problem where I needed to change a bank account number. This change effected all of my accounts connected to this one bank account, from my transfer capabilities to my paycheck being deposited. I forgot one of my accounts and had to scramble to update it when I discovered it. It took a while to get everything worked out and running smoothly again. Have you yet to reconnect your PayPal or other accounts with the new account number?

❑ Are you still using stamps when BillPay is a free option with your bank? Time to set it up! Do you need to add any new billers? Do you need to delete any old ones?

❑ Update your payment systems - Do you use PayPal, Venmo, or Square? Are they set up properly? Do you also have a business PayPal account to update? Ensure it is working properly or you will miss out on payments. Do you need to pull accounting reports but haven't quite figured out how? Now is the time to get yourself familiar with these features.

❑ Does your PayPal account still have your maiden name and yet you've just celebrated your eighteenth wedding anniversary? This small detail makes it complicated for you to receive packages using PayPal, missing out on deliveries, reimbursements for non-delivery policies, etc. Clearing up small details such as these in all of your financial accounts will make your life run much smoother.

Budgets and Accounting:
What is your financial goal by having an accounting program? Is it compatible with your future financial goals, such as buying a home, maintaining your business, or finding the funds to splurge on that 7500-piece Millennium Falcon LEGO set you've been drooling over?

❏ Update your accounting app up - For both security reasons and for the best features, be sure you have updated and backed up the accounting information.

❏ Are you happy with your accounting app? Does it help you reach your financial goals? Do you have all of your accounts listed as they need to be for it to be a helpful accounting program? Have you set it up properly for your best use? If you haven't used it, why not? Too confusing? Check the software forums to help you break through the confusion. Keeping track of your income and expenses to ensure you properly allocate your funds is important. Using any one of the several accounting options available to you can be tricky work. We each have different accounting needs and prefer different interface options.

❏ How are you digitally accounting for your online income? There is a wide variety of digital accounting options for both personal and business, such as Quicken, QuickBooks, FreshBooks, Mint, or simply a spreadsheet of your own making. No matter your preferred choice, it's time to right-size your accounting options.

So many tiny details go into all of the financial mechanics these days, so you need to be vigilant. Be judicious in the accounts you set up.

❏ Are you up to date with the entries? This is a task that needs regular maintenance, so setting up a regular day and block of time each week makes it much easier to ensure you are on top of your finances. I tackle this mundane task in my "Money Monday" block of time.

❏ Are you still using the accounting program? Subscription programs that give you money management info but are actually sucking your money away bit by bit each month need to be canceled. Mark when the subscription ends or is up for renewal, and take action before it does!

If they've been truly helpful, keep going with them. Seeing all of your finances in a single place can give you a great picture of your financial health.

Credit cards:
Are you paying them off in the most advantageous order? Check their interest rates, and pay off your highest interest rates first. Do you know all of the accounts each credit card is connected to? Be sure to have an accurate list of which digital accounts are attached to which credit cards in case the card is lost or stolen. Do you need to make changes to these accounts, such as moving some accounts to a different credit card like a business credit card?

Loans:
Many loans, such as a mortgage, personal loans, auto loans, student loans, etc., offer a small discount if you make the payments electronically. This means giving permission for the creditor to pull the funds from your account electronically.
❏ Ensure your accounts are running smoothly so you do not lose out on the special discount offered.
❏ Check each account to confirm your loan company is properly crediting your payments within your loan accounts. All of this information is usually available to confirm online.

Insurance:
Most of you have several different types of insurance, some of which may be health, homeowner's, renter's, auto insurance, liability, or even pet insurance.

Do they need to be set up in BillPay? Are they on Autopay? Is this the right choice for you?

Health care:
A lot of healthcare in the United States is managed digitally. From your insurance to how you receive your CT Scans, it all sits out there on the internet behind a password. Here are a few more prompts to organize your digital financial life; gather each that applies to you, set it up, or eliminate as needed.

❑ Health insurance - Don't forget to keep a digital copy of your health insurance card for emergency purposes.

❑ HSA - Health Savings Accounts

❑ FSA - Flex Spending Accounts

❑ Hospital networks, clinics, doctor's offices, and dentists all seem to expect you to sign up for their own network to receive messages. I enjoy receiving my CT Scans and X-rays from my appointments. As an artist, I have taken several of these diagnostic tools and transformed them into artworks, moving difficult medical situations into educational and therapeutic actions.
Oh, and this same portal is usually used to pay bills electronically. Every single one has its own account with its own passwords. Yes, more pain after the original pain of the appointment!

Education:
❑ Homework portals
❑ Tuitions payments
❑ Digital textbooks
❑ 529 Plans
❑ FAFSA

More accounts, more passwords, more of you and your family's life online that you need to keep track of. Periodically check that all accounts are up to date, along with funds and information moving smoothly where they need to go.

Renewals and subscriptions:
❑ List each of your digital subscriptions - Add up all the digital subscriptions you pay for. List which accounts are connected with which credit card. I have a list of all of my digital subscriptions in my favorite note-taking app.

I was always forgetting one or two subscriptions, so I created a list in my favorite note-taking app in the cloud to remind me exactly which accounts I have attached to which credit card. When a credit card expires or has been stolen, we need to go through all of the accounts we have attached to that credit card and update it with the new card information.

Have this information available in the cloud as you may need the information when you are away from home. Credit cards or their information are often stolen when traveling, and if a replacement can arrive while you are still traveling, this information is vital to keep your accounts up to date. I can go down the list one by one and update the information.

Referencing the credit card bill wasn't helpful as not all the accounts attached were visible in the previous couple of months.

❑ Monthly and annual accounts - Some accounts renew monthly, such as Netflix or a gym membership, and others are charged annually, such as accounting software and magazines.

Ask yourself, do you need each one? Do you still want to pay the price you are paying for the subscription? Is there a less expensive pricing option available? Or do you need the more expensive package to continue enjoying the subscription?

PRO TIP: Set up reminders on your smartphone, digital calendar, or in a note-taking app such as Evernote to renew or cancel your unneeded subscriptions. Make conscious decisions regarding each renewal . . . too often you'll see a renewal has already been charged when you were already thinking about canceling. Then you just let it ride and maybe not even use the service as you have forgotten about it, again. This will ensure you either renew with a happy yes or cancel your unnecessary subscriptions.

❑ Pay special attention to your various subscription services such as Adobe Creative Cloud. Customers store a huge amount of digital assets behind their 100GB paywall. That would be a lot of work lost!

❑ Business with Amazon, Etsy, etc. - In your excitement to get your latest app up and ready for sale or your jewelry business up on Etsy, you'll often overlook the small financial details—the little gotchas in the fine print.

Check the latest rates on the various websites and their payment systems. Have they changed since you established your business and set your product prices? You may find a more advantageous pricing system with the newest upgrades. Make changes as necessary.

❑ Retail accounts:
Shoes, Clothing, Sports, Auto parts, Sheet music . . . the options are endless. The more hobbies you and your family have, the longer the list of retail accounts you will likely have. Sometimes you prefer to have the company store your credit card, such as Amazon, so it's easier each time you purchase another eBook.

Retirement:
❑ Are you happy with how your retirement accounts are set up? Is there any business you need to complete such as naming your beneficiaries? Do you need to update the account for automatic contributions or distributions?

❑ Stocks, Dividends - Update your allocation.

❑ Bitcoin

❑ Taxes - It comes around every year. Are you ready for it this year? If you are in business, you may need to file taxes quarterly.

❑ Individual IRAs and Taxes - If it is the last days before tax returns are due to be filed in the States and the last days before you can place the previous year's funds into an Individual IRA, don't wait until the last minute to file online, just in case there is a glitch in the system.

❑ Credit reports - Yes, these also. Each company's report needs to be periodically monitored. And yes, that will require more passwords that need to be created and maintained.

❑ Check-in: Security and Password Management - Managing your digital life feels more like accumulating passwords. Do we get badges or bonuses for every five passwords? Nope, although properly accumulating them does save us time in the long run. You are still applying your password system from Chapter 12, right?

I am in the habit of working on at least one task each week on "Money Mondays," which can be as many as 52 items done each year! Now it is easier to see the true cost and income of your digital footprint and make changes that right-size your digital life for you, your business, and your family.

24 - Audio

Music sets the mood of our lives, from quiet study sessions to the loudest of rock concerts. Some of you enjoy every aspect of music, from listening to playing an instrument, including producing music. This means there is a lot of music to organize. Even if you aren't selling your music, having sheet music accounts and files of composition notes on various devices can be confusing.

Listening:
❑ Radio apps - Go through each of your music apps on each of your devices and create the best music experience for your needs. Does your phone have the music you want to hear? Do your radio apps have your favorite channels set? Different devices have a slightly different collection on each device. I have an old smartphone set up on my Bluetooth speakers that stays in my office serving as a permanent radio. Set your music for your needs on each of your devices, in each of the areas you live in.

❑ Set your favorite channels - XM Radio, TuneIn, Spotify, and other radio apps

❑ Music Accounts - Right-size your music accounts. There are several great choices for listening to music. Calculate how much you are spending on these music channels. Now that you have gone through all of your music accounts and see what you have and how much they are costing you per month, what other options are available? Are you getting your money's worth from the ones you pay for, or is there a new and better way to enjoy your favorite music? Is it too much on the wrong channels? Can you consolidate to just one or do you need to change due to your growing family to one that pays for a wider range of options?

❏ Gift Cards - Do you have iTunes or GooglePlay gift cards you've forgotten to load to your account? I had to Google how to do so for my iTunes account. Are there any other gift cards you need to be using? Amazon? LINE? Check the amount of funds available on the ones you aren't interested in and see about forwarding them to someone who would appreciate the product. Be careful as some cards charge a fee if you don't use them.

❏ Spotify - Curate the artists and playlists you follow. Update your settings including your privacy settings.

Check the music accounts that come with your computer's operating system such as -
❏ iTunes
❏ Google Play
❏ Open Source

❏ Bluetooth Speaker - Is your Bluetooth speaker system set up and working for you as it should? Are there problems with the connection? Does an update need to be made for it to work again? Is it in the room you use the most?

❏ Stereo system, in-home theater system setup - Do you need to finish setting it up properly? Does it need to be reconfigured since the living room was rearranged?

❏ Earphones and earbuds - Are they connecting to your device properly? Does your current pair have a cord that's getting mangled and you should replace them?
Is the charging station convenient for your wireless earbuds?

Playing an instrument:
- ❑ Tuning apps
- ❑ Metronome app
- ❑ Digital Sheet Music Accounts

Producing:
- ❑ Audio software
- ❑ Stitcher
- ❑ GarageBand, Digital Recording, Bandcamp
- ❑ Music accounts for use on Podcasts and YouTube videos such as, Creative Commons, or Epidemic Music.

Audio is so much more than music; it's also audiobooks, podcasts, and the equipment you use to make them happen—both listening with earphones and recording through microphones.

❑ Website - Is your website set up for your audio needs? Are you having trouble connecting your Soundcloud account to your website? Are you having problems with your website loading properly with sound and video? Is it the right website package? Do you need to upgrade because you are running out of data storage?

❑ Check your music sales setup - Are clips for potential clients to hire you easy to find on your website? Is everything working correctly for clients to purchase your music from all of your checkout points? Do they load quickly enough? Many of us wait only three seconds or so before we move on to a more quickly loading website.

❑ Podcasts (audio) apps - I have yet to find an audio app that I'm happy with. I have my list of podcasts and try to listen to them as much as possible, but then I find I have a list of half-listened-to episodes and have a hard time finding where I left off when I return two weeks later. It's only after starting yet another new episode that it then jumps to the previously unfinished episode instead of the next new episode on the list.

It took a while to figure out an app I like to use. The original podcast app that comes installed on the iPhone keeps downloading more episodes than I want, and I found it took up a large amount of memory on my phone. I deleted this disappointing podcast app. Now I'll sometimes use Soundcloud or Overcast. How are you listening to podcasts?

❑ Family-friendly podcasts - Mark your favorite family-friendly podcast. Great for kids to listen to on those yucky rainy days, the snow days, or the super-hot days during summer. My grandmother would make fun, indoor camping events for us grandkids when we were sick. Make the most miserable of sick days just a little bit better with a good podcast.

❑ Podcast Producers - Time to check your equipment for proper maintenance. Are your audio podcasts easy to find and play? Are you available on multiple platforms for clients to listen to as they feel most comfortable? Are there any glitches you need to fix to get your listening numbers up? Do you need new equipment? Better post-processing software?

❑ AudioBooks - For those times when we can't just sit and read a book, AudioBooks have been a great substitute. They fill our commutes with great stories and new knowledge. My studio work time is also filled with mystery and laughter while producing a great bit of artwork. I enjoy listening to audiobooks through Open Culture, too. We don't have time to waste on a bad book, nor do we have time to finish bad audiobooks. Delete the ones you'll never finish.

❑ Family AudioBooks - Is your family up for listening to great audiobooks including fun short stories or ghost stories around a campfire on a dark evening? A good respite from screen time is to have a story read aloud.

❑ Bloggers - Do you offer an option for the blind to listen to your blog posts? Reading your blog posts and posting the audio clip within your blog post adds an entirely new dimension to your website. Offering bonus content can really draw more fans into more of your product offerings.

❑ Check-in: Having trouble sticking with the mind-numbing email decluttering each day or the thousands of photos you are organizing? What is the length of your favorite song or album? Challenge yourself to declutter for the length of that song. Then challenge yourself to play the song twice. Next, challenge yourself to declutter to the whole album.

Take control of the soundtrack of your life. Keep the music you love, the music that inspires you, the podcast that moves you, and the audiobook that relaxes you. Don't waste data space and your time on music or audiobooks that don't fulfill you. Make the playlists that wake you up in the morning and the ones that relax you in the evening. It's your life; organize it as you want to live it!

25 - Movies & Video

The market for television viewing, sports leagues, and movies is becoming crowded as more and more media companies are building their own streaming services. We used to have limited choices on how to watch TV, sports, and movies. Now, however, your many options can become just another media player to easily bring you top-rated shows to your television through a multitude of devices for your viewing pleasure.

But really, how much media do you need? How much time in your busy schedule do you have to watch the thousands of hours you currently have available for streaming into your home? Are you overpaying for media access in your home? You need to work, take care of your family, and handle other responsibilities. Movie night once or twice a week is great, but have you found yourselves sitting on the couch night after night consuming media, deciding not to work out or make tomorrow's lunch ahead of time?

In addition to your online classes, listening to music, gaming, and all your other activities, how much TV can you watch? How many hours each week do you want to devote to your TV viewing?

❑ Movie Nights! Edit your watch list - While the popcorn is popping and the drinks are being prepared, edit your watch list. Go

through the family Netflix "Watch Later" list. Will you watch one of those movies tonight?
❑ Choose a movie that is sitting on the list and remove it when you've finished.
❑ Delete movies you've lost interest in watching.

❑ As you edit your personally compiled note of "Recommended Watching" or the in-app offered "Wish List," look at how much you still want to watch. Is it a mediocre list of, "Well, if I can't find anything better tonight?" Or do you have limited time to view that movie before it is deleted from Netflix's movie library?

❑ Each movie night, choose a different media company in which to cull the viewing list . . . Netflix, Hulu, Prime, etc.

❑ Time to cancel or change your level of service.
When you go through each media option you already subscribe to, does it still contain the content you want to continue watching? Compare it to others you are also paying for. Which service provides the best content for your money? Are you finding one service is grabbing your attention much more consistently? Which one does your family prefer?

Right-size your services, declutter your media - Delete the extra options you rarely view. Add the media you do want, including the media and video your children need.

❑ Apple+
❑ BritBox/Acorn
❑ Disney
❑ Hulu
❑ MLB, sports leagues
❑ Netflix
❑ Amazon Prime

❑ Home Theater System
❑ Apple TV
❑ PlayStation, Nintendo
❑ Amazon Echo, Google Assistant

❏ Curate the movies and videos on your portable devices - Where are your movies and television shows? Time to put the right apps on the right devices. Check how much space is left on your smartphone or tablet. Can the right movies be accessed via the right device? Watch the amount of GBs available on your device. Also, note that downloading a movie from iTunes to your iPad does not count against your iCloud data GB. It is handled differently by Apple than your photographs, work proposals, and personal videos. Take a few minutes to refresh your movie and TV show options on your devices.

Before a long trip, I always load my phone with a movie or two and a couple of podcasts. I like to listen to something as I get other work done—it gives me the satisfaction of accomplishing something at a time when I feel my life is put on hold.

Unfortunately, I often forget that I've added the media when I return home, and they stay there, taking up a huge amount of space. Then I'm recording a video of something and suddenly receive a warning that I have no more space on my phone!

❏ I have the Netflix app on one device yet not on another device as they each have different uses. Some movies and TV shows are downloaded on one device and not others, and too often I realize I'd prefer to watch Netflix on the tablet instead of my smartphone and am stuck on the train or a plane wanting to see the movie from the other device.

Video streaming onto every one of our devices is now ubiquitous and can be overwhelming if we are not careful. Make smart choices as to which subscriptions give you the most entertainment, education, and laughs for your money. They don't all need to be on every device. Take control of what you watch and where you watch it.

❏ Curate your own video collection - Videos you create are the biggest data hogs, and you really need to go through them often. After events such as a wedding, don't forget, as mentioned in Chapter 16, to schedule the time to go through the photos and videos accumulated from it. The couple would probably appreciate another point of view of their event, and you can truly feel the event is done and move on to the next.

When I create an artwork, I don't feel it is a completed piece until it is framed and ready for sale. When I return from holidays, I schedule time to go through the photos and videos to cull the excess, file the best ones, and create little videos to share of the event.

Check-in: Include a bit of simple maintenance to complete during a captive decluttering session. Have you accumulated more new apps since the last time you went through and culled the ones you don't use? Remember that you can download them again if you decide you really want to keep it, but until then, just get this extra clutter off your phone. Simple maintenance such as this during your captive decluttering times will help you stay efficient.

Three-step mini Checklist:
❏ Declutter any new stray apps that you have tried and rejected since beginning your decluttering process.
❏ Update your notifications - New apps means new notifications; make adjustments as needed.
❏ Rearrange new apps - Any new apps you choose to keep on your devices may need to be moved to a better location to maintain organization.

26 - Reading

I am addicted to reading books and have been my whole life. I remember reading books in my bedroom by the nightlight down the hall after lights out. I continue to go to great lengths to ensure I always have access to reading material wherever I am. Visiting bookstores and frequenting libraries is a bone-deep need in my soul.

As a voracious reader, I found living in Japan that I could no longer just run to the library for new books, nor could I find the big selections of books I could read easily at my local bookstore. This made it a major event in my life to visit the three used English bookstores available at the time in the Tokyo Bay area, bringing my huge wheelie suitcase on the train to buy as many books as were on my long lists and seeking new authors to take me on new adventures.

❏ eBooks - Digital declutter as a reader. My current go-to "book" is my smartphone, and I have over 1500 books available at my fingertips through my reading apps. Over the years, these reading apps have continued to improve, and many of the features are essential to comfortable reading. Is your reading app set just right for you to enjoy reading your favorite books? Make adjustments to your reader for the most comfortable reading experience.

❑ Set the background and your font preferences - Choose the settings that are most comfortable for your eyes. Mine is set to a black background with large, white lettering and is most comfortable on my eyes especially at night when going to sleep. The black background is also helpful to prolong the smartphone's battery life.

❑ Adjust the font size best for your eyes - The font style is changeable, too, as is the way one can scroll through the book. One can flip through the pages or one can infinitely scroll like it is an Instagram feed.

❑ Magazine and newspaper subscriptions - I enjoy reading fiction on my smartphone, but I prefer to read non-fiction and magazines on my tablet or in paper form. Old magazines downloaded onto my tablet have accumulated in the app that I don't need to have anymore. Are your subscriptions on auto-renew? Do you continue to read them consistently and enjoy the subscriptions? I had a couple of magazines on auto-renew and I realized that I never received or missed the message when a new issue arrived on my Kindle. Then I also realized I was three issues behind and found I was not really that excited about subscribing to these magazines. I've decided I don't want to receive those anymore, so now I'm searching for how to cancel. It is a big search on the site that now needs a Google search. I've already paid for the full year automatically, so I'm not sure if I'll get a portion of that back or not. The best I've found is to mark an appointment with my calendar a bit before it renews and catch it then. How many magazines or newspapers do you have on auto-renew?

❑ Cull your magazine and newspaper subscriptions - Do you want to continue with the service? Do you need to cancel others? You can see which subscriptions remain unopened. You only have so much time in your days. Delete any you don't want anymore, and take notes on the one article or two you'd like to remember and keep it in your favorite note-taking app.

❑ One of the eReader apps on my tablet has also become the

dumping ground for most of my pdf files that need to be read or saved for whatever reason. From instruction books to patterns to writings you have been requested to edit, it just piles up there if you don't specifically take the time to cull it. It can lead to a surprisingly large amount of data if you're not careful. Too often I wait to delete them "just in case" and still have them over a year later. Not anymore. File them in a note-taking app or delete it. Now, this is a huge pile of everything as it's what I use to read all other pdf files, Open Culture books, sheet music for my keyboard, application forms, knitting patterns, cookbooks by others, a cookbook rough draft I've written, project proposals, and a general mish-mash of every aspect of my life. Not sure why there is a flight ticket in there, but this definitely needs a bulldozer bit of organizing. It even includes my keyboard instruction book. Yes, I still need it.

❏ Account set up - Do you need to set up new accounts for additional family members? Or cancel others? Do you have any gift cards you need to add from places like Amazon or Barnes & Noble?

❏ Blogs and news - Go through your RSS reader app, such as Feedly, and see if you can consolidate them all into a single preferred app. I love my Feedly RSS reader, which keeps my click circuit travels short. My reader is set up to bring all of the sites I want to keep current on within a single place, from the stock market and business information to the blog of a great fiber artist in Maryland. I can see it all, chronologically from the last several days since I checked. Many of my favorite websites, news, and blogs come to me in this single app.

❏ Check accounts you follow in your RSS reader - Several may have chosen to no longer post anything, and some may have chosen to move in another direction that you no longer find beneficial. What about the direction in which you have been moving? New activities or a job change will alter your interests, and you'll now prefer to follow different content. Update your list and stay on top of the happenings in your new industry and evolving hobbies.

❑ Edit your eReader apps - Are you jumping between different apps and have some books on one app, some on another, and it takes you awhile to find what you need? Can you choose one app and choose books from this single app moving forward?

❑ Education - Are old textbooks and homework you no longer need still on your eBook app? If it's near the end of the school year and finals will be happening soon, help your focus by offloading all the extra old textbooks and old homework. My iBooks App is filled with random PDFs, residency applications, keyboard music, and rough drafts for project proposals.

❑ Should you be adding several more eBook apps as your children have advanced with their reading abilities? Are they getting old enough to have their own accounts? Are you, your ereader, and the children ready for the summer-reading list?

❑ Goodreads is a good way to find new title recommendations and keep a record for yourself of how many books you have read and to place your own reviews.

❑ Your local library - Americans visited the library more than twice as often as they went to the movies according to a Gallup poll conducted in December of 2019. Borrow books and other media for free from your local library. Return the items before the due date and you're then welcome to borrow more! Such an amazing deal.

❑ Sign up to have your entire family signed on as members of your local library - Many libraries have fun summer-reading events and more for the children in addition to eBooks available. There are also other media available that can be checked out for watching or listening at home depending on your local library. Libraries have been offering ebooks to check out for a while now. They are such a great resource to borrow books for free, and with a quick online return, you can borrow even more! Visit your local library website to find out how to set up for e-check-out for eBooks, newspaper subscriptions, and more. Libraries also have computers and the internet for you to get work done.

- [ ] Library apps e.g. Overdrive app - Load it on your phone or tablet. It's the standard app to use for library ebooks in the US.

- [ ] Consolidate your writing - Many of us are not just consumers of words but creators of books ourselves. How is this going? Should you step up and purchase a better writing program? Is your latest book still in pieces between multiple programs and needs to be consolidated? Do you need to update how these are organized so you can easily find and access them?

- [ ] Writers - Is your website set up for your fans to easily purchase and download your latest books, articles, blogs, or newsletters? We are all busy and impatient, so ensure that your page loads quickly and your newest and best-sellers are front and center.

- [ ] Can you dictate your book, blog, notes, or articles on your commute? I write and edit on my phone while I commute by train. It's also a good time to do research, so a good digital note-taking flow is essential.

- [ ] Specialized blogs - Patreon and Medium are an additional kind of subscription that we need to take time to read, and we often pay for this privilege. Eliminating some subscriptions can open up the option to provide more funds to your favorites.

We are each going to have a unique load of reading materials in random corners of our digital life. That's okay; now is your chance to clean it up and organize it with your priorities in mind.

Check-in: Are you keeping with your decluttering habits? Making appointments with yourself to keep the habit will help you form the habit. Consistently scheduling your habits with yourself is really important for your follow-through. You are the most important person you need to keep appointments with. A weekly check-in with yourself is a comfortable timeframe, and it gives you a chance to go over what you have accomplished, analyze what didn't go well and why along with making plans and adjustments for the coming week ahead. This small weekly check-in with myself helps keep me on track with my most important things, from meal planning to appointments. I need to ensure I keep my tasks focused on my long-term goals and make room for good times with friends and family. Usually, one hour on Sunday evening or early Monday morning is enough time to plot my progress and keep a relaxed pace moving forward.

27 - Note-taking Apps

As you move through *The BIG Checklist,* look at how much work you have already completed and how much less cluttered your devices are. Keeping the digital decluttering habit throughout the different chapters in a consistent timed or task-oriented habit makes a big difference.

Using note-taking apps to declutter and improve your note-taking flow is now a timed task in your AM launch or evening setup.

Note-taking apps such as Evernote, OneNote, and Notion are productivity apps meant to make things easier for you. For those of you who take notes and like to keep records of things, these note-taking apps are amazing! You no longer need to keep a big filing cabinet or two in your home. You can be organized and efficient without the need for extra furniture and clutter in your office space.

I love my note-taking app! It's like my very own office library with all of the information that would normally be included in those cumbersome filing cabinets in an office. Now I can neatly tuck it all away in a Notes or Evernote app.

What was once stacks of papers piled high on top of your already overflowing desk is now hidden within the depths of your digital clutter. In either place, it's still difficult to find. Time to break big tasks like the entirety of your note-taking app into smaller bites to help you see that you are making progress.

Between the free apps available with each operating system, such as Notes or OneNote, or the Google Keep option, and then the pay app options such as Evernote, you have found yourself with notes all over the place.

There is a note-taking app for almost every personality out there. Even those of you who prefer to use paper to take notes, you often find yourselves then scanning or photographing the note for later use.

You have personal notes, family notes, and business notes all across several platforms. Apple's notes, Google's notes, and Dropbox for connecting and coworking leave us with a scattered mess as much as any paper note hoarder!

You have a small collection of productivity and organizing apps! They must be small . . . they all fit on your smartphone, right? You have high hopes that your busy life will become miraculously organized and hyper-productive with each app you download. Each book you read or podcast you listen to gives you more ideas and tells you it's a better way to connect with others. Choose which apps are working best for your personal and business needs and delete the rest.

❑ Consolidate your note-taking apps - I had more than one note-taking app for a short time, and the back and forth was incredibly cumbersome. It became a confusing mess! I had big projects in one and grocery lists in another, and soon they got mixed together and I had to take command of my notes. Of all the options, choose the one you prefer and stick with it. Delete the note-taking apps that are too cumbersome and inefficient for your life.

It's your consistency of actions that help propel your productivity efforts forward. Be prudent in the efficiency apps in which you keep.

PRO Tip: Just like photos and emails, tackle the oldest notes and the oldest notebooks first. If you need to break down some notebooks into additional smaller notebooks such as by year to reach your goal, then do so.

❏ Visit each notebook, one by one, to be sure it is valuable enough to keep, taking up precious data space. Start with either the oldest projects first or start with the smallest folder, the low-hanging fruit, to give yourself the strongest jump-start into decluttering your note app. Make sure all your notes are in their proper folders or notebooks. Some notes are definite keepers, and yet other notes seem to have been written by a mysterious, much more interesting alter ego.

Within each note make the decision to:
❏ Keep
❏ Edit and consolidate. Be sure to take into consideration anyone you are sharing the note with. Will they need to access the note in the future? Send them a polite note informing them of your intention to archive or delete the notes with a deadline for them to access the note.
❏ Archive - Some projects have long been completed and you no longer need evidence of your hand in it, so that can be deleted. Some do need to be kept, but some of the notes can be consolidated or deleted to only its essentials.
❏ Delete

❏ Create a dashboard or index note with hot links to other notes and notebooks for quick and easy access.

❏ Make several dashboards if you have multiple notes and notebooks you need quick access to.

❏ Declutter the app's default miscellaneous notebook - There is a catch-all place in note apps that needs to be properly filed away or deleted. This is the one notebook or folder that is the repository for all the miscellaneous notes that open. It's filled with random bits you've taken of someone's contact info, a photo of a recipe, and an email you've forwarded into your notes program.

❏ Create an "Actions" notebook - This is my default notebook that keeps my quickly accessed notes, which are then properly refiled during my evening setup time. It is in my "Actions" notebook—that I keep my grocery list, current to-do list, current residency applications, and other items on which I literally need to take action quickly. It's the notebook I access several times each day.

How many abandoned, unsorted notes do you have? My solution is to have a specific "Action" notebook that it opens to. Any miscellaneous note I start automatically goes into my "Action" file. I only need to check one file or notebook for stray notes for proper filing. No need to hunt them down. Before I specified this "Action" note, I would forget to move miscellaneous notes to the correct file; it would just sit in the default file until I no longer had any idea what it meant. Break this big task down into small bites. We'll look at that one notebook that is our initial contact with our note-taking app.

I have been using Evernote for years and have been happy with its system. Its upgrades have grown as my note-keeping needs have grown. The cookbook I wrote five years ago was still there when I was ready to complete it.

Each note-taking app has its own personality, so choose the one that fits you and your lifestyle. Yes, it does sound like a relationship, because it is. Considering how much time we spend with our computers and our apps, we need to feel comfortable with the relationship we have with them.

If you have vital information you don't want to lose, I recommend using a secondary note-taking system as a backup, but keep your favorite as a working note-taking app.

❏ Check your features - Are you taking advantage of everything in the app that would be helpful for you?

❏ Right-size your note-taking app - Are you paying for the right level of service? If yes, that's great, but is it worth the extra money you pay for one of the pay options? Do you need more service from your current note-taking app? Consider note-taking apps for both your business needs and personal life. With dozens of notebooks and the notes multiplying out from there, this needs to be digitally decluttered.

❏ Tag your notes - Tag your notes so you can find them easily again. Search functions are getting better and better, but tagging ensures you will not lose that one small note among the thousands of others.

❏ Delete the old scrappy notes you no longer need.
❏ Create new notebooks for new groups of notes that need to be organized.
❏ File the notes you wish to keep into their proper notebooks or folders.

❏ Combine your notebooks - It's like creating your own box set or omnibus. Your notes are pages that go into notebooks, and then the notebooks are stacked together into an even more consolidated box set. Should any of your notebooks become part of a larger stack of books? For example, each proposal I create is filled with notes, which becomes a notebook. Then I stack all the notebooks of proposals together, which is an archive of proposals I can access for future reference. Therefore I am reducing the number of notebooks to see when I open my note app.

❏ Decompile notebooks - Do you need to rearrange your stacks of notebooks into different stacks or completely decouple any notebooks?

❏ Set up email forwarding - Is your note-taking app set up for you to send emails directly to it? There are some emails I want to keep in another place, and being able to forward that email directly to the project notebook is extremely convenient. Learn how adding the correct tags to the subject line allows the email to go directly into the notebook you want it to go. Adding proper tagging information in the subject line of emails can send those emails to the very specific folder you want it to go to, completely eliminating the need to go through the app's miscellaneous default folder.

❏ Remember your captive decluttering times - Is your note-taking app set up on your devices for you to accomplish captive decluttering? Are you able to go through your phone and edit notes as you move throughout your day?

❏ Scanning and tagging - Scanning documents into your note-taking app is super convenient, and tagging each scan will help with your future searches. Adding this information into notes is quite easy and important as scanned information isn't always read by the note app's search engine. Double-check your note apps capabilities. Is the readability of scanned items a higher pay level?

Remember, as mentioned in Chapter 10, that using the search function can often be faster than clicking through to all the folders and subfolders to get to the note you need.

This is best done as a timed task to nibble away at its excess over the next couple of weeks or months depending on how prolific your note-taking is. On a recent screen share, I saw someone who had over 36,000 notes!

❏ What is saved in your note cloud? - I use mine as a library for quick referencing of today's to-do list, tomorrow's grocery list, proposals for the next couple of weeks, and 90-day projects. Books go in and are sometimes not accessed until five or six years later when I'm ready to tackle that cookbook project again. Many are simply archived, such as an art proposal from six years ago, or family reunion meal planning notes, or ski trip vacation details that will be handy when you return next year.

I have a lot out there in the cloud, a lot of which I have forgotten about, too. Just a quick look through my notes and I see a few that I just have no idea what I would have saved it for, and some that are just so mysterious I think that aliens came by in the middle of the night and typed them into my account.

Check out the following prompts to help you see some areas of your life where you could be more digitally organized.
- ❏ Travel plans and miles programs
- ❏ Family calendar - All the family and friends' birthdays, wedding anniversaries, etc. Update your current system . . . or try a new system for a week or two and get feedback from your family.
- ❏ Hobbies - woodworking and sewing notes
- ❏ Wedding plans
- ❏ House inventory - Archived photos, scans of receipts, and notes of your possessions for insurance purposes
- ❏ Comparing the pros and cons of the latest fishing gear
- ❏ Workout and fitness notes, triathlon race options
- ❏ Photographs from old creative projects, archiving to prove your idea progression
- ❏ Art exhibition labels
- ❏ Applications, grants, jobs
- ❏ Class notes, school assignments
- ❏ Forwarded emails
- ❏ Scanned receipts
- ❏ School information

❏ Cookbook notebook - I prefer to read non-fiction books in their paper form, but recipes are small pieces of information that I collect one at a time. I have scans of heirloom family recipes originally written on recipe cards. I have typed recipes that link to their corresponding YouTube video demonstrations. For recipes I create myself, I also have photographs of various ingredients and of the final delicious result.

❏ Share family recipes and history - Now that you have organized and collected family recipes and other historical information, your family may appreciate access to it to pass on to new generations. Share the family cookbook notes with them. Ask other family members to contribute to the notebook to give a more complete picture of your family.

❏ Podcasts - I have a running list of podcasts I receive recommendations for divided into two lists. One list is podcasts to watch, the second is podcasts to listen to. Update your list as you work your way through it. Are you still interested or are you no longer planning to bring in goats for lawn maintenance?

Do not be intimidated by the quantity. Make a choice to tackle each notebook via timed or task-specific challenges. I have consolidated one or two of my favorite time-management systems into a couple of features and now use an amalgamation of these into a single system that is most efficient for my lifestyle. A bit of Pomodoro here, a bit of KonMari there, and voila, my life is an efficient, organized work of art. Completing the decluttering for each notebook, one by one, will take time, energy, and good habits to complete this long-term project. Completing the task notebook by notebook will provide systematic and more manageable-sized pieces to declutter.

28 - Professional Software

The amount of professional software available feels limitless and spans the range of almost every industry across the planet. I'll touch on a few popular ones for you to get a good idea of how to proceed with decluttering your own industry's niche programs.

Unique software pervades almost every industry. I couldn't begin to cover even a fraction of them in this digital declutter checklist, so I have set aside this chapter for you, the expert in your field, to take command by creating your own checklist for the software you use. We've been working through *The BIG Checklist*, so you have a good idea about what you need to do.

No matter your industry, your digital work schedule and your digital calendar are paramount to using your time most productively. Programs such as iCal and Google Calendar are ubiquitous, but creating your own in an app such as Evernote works also and needs to be updated and maintained regularly.

❑ Declutter your digital schedule so it works for you - Update the system of tags you are using. What annoying glitches are you stuck inside?

It took a while for me to figure out how to deal with work and meetings in different time zones. Research your way out of that, or maybe now is the time to migrate to a different program.

Start with the software and apps included with your computer purchase. Time to concentrate on the professional software that is part of your computer. You most likely have a spreadsheet program, a word-writing program, and a PowerPoint or Keynote presentation program on your computer.

❏ Update the software - To capture the newest features and security settings, be sure all the software is up to date.

❏ Dig into each program one at a time. Spend time on one each day. If you have a huge backlog of files, take several days or a week for each. Start with a search for duplicate files. Each program's decluttering needs will be slightly different, so mark your specific needs in your schedule for future maintenance.

❏ Organize your decluttering into smaller folders by event, date, or project and take smaller bites of the decluttering tasks.

PRO Tip: Some projects have teams working on a large, centralized file. Tackle the decluttering together as a team to get it done faster and you'll be less likely to overlook important documents.

❏ Check the professional software you have added after your purchase. For example, Microsoft apps may have been added to your Apple computers.

❏ Project management software - Does your company use Slack, G-Suite, Asana, or other similar software? I signed up for Slack as part of a group project a couple of years ago and haven't used it since. None of my group projects since have used it. And yet, it is sitting on both my computer and smartphone, taking up space. Time to delete. If I need it again in the future, there will be a time and place. I still have the sign-in info, so I can reload it—a simple enough action. How many of these types of apps do you have cluttering your devices?

❑ Delete downloaded apps that are not an asset to your organization. Did Slack work but not Trello, or vice versa? Make more room for the ones that work. Sometimes the newest, and latest whizbang app is a great step in the right direction for your organization. It's amazing when it works out, but sometimes it doesn't.

For this chapter, as an example of professional software, I'll be using Adobe Creative Cloud, from their free smartphone and tablet app options used to edit family and Instagram photographs to their full-price package options used by the multi-billion-dollar movie industry. I believe it will help give a clear picture of how a smooth, uncluttered workflow is worth the time and effort.

I am still learning the workflow as Adobe continues to make marked improvements for ease of use. The more I use it, the more useful it becomes for me. When I get to a point of frustration and wonder if I'm doing something wrong or wondering why I can't find a certain feature, I discover that Adobe has been working on exactly that problem and is now releasing a simple solution.

In the meantime, I had eight different files of the same image saved but only slightly different experiments, and then I had to figure out which one I wanted to use yet be sure I saved the original.

❑ Organize files and folders - Adobe Creative Cloud sounds so simple until you realize there are multiple folders and files in which to place things in the cloud. Some are libraries, some are files, but all are assets, and it can get confusing. Is it getting to the point where you are losing some of your digital assets in folders you didn't even know existed? Many software programs have their quirks, and you're likely not the first to do a search for answers.

❑ Organize library - Yes, your digital assets in the library are different from your digital assets in your folders. Moving them isn't always an option; neither is renaming them unless they are moved into another folder first. As with all programs, it has its quirks.

❑ Save As - Learn where your files are saved to. Multiple apps rename your digital files and sometimes send things to hard-to-find places.

❏ Update each app you use regularly - There are a large number of apps available under the Adobe CC subscription, so be sure to take advantage of as many of them as possible. When I use them on my laptop, they need to be updated to receive the latest features.

❏ Update your profile - Remember, this is a worldwide, creative-industry-used software program, so a lot of industry connections and opportunities are made through Adobe's Portfolio and Behance options available with their subscription service. Many use it for business, from small business marketers to large corporations. It's vital to present your brand well and be able to contact and respond quickly to requests.

❏ Double-check when deleting digital assets - How does your industry's software handle assets that are moved to the trash bin? Creative Cloud has a safety net when you delete your assets. It doesn't permanently delete until you go into your delete folder and specifically request those assets to be deleted permanently. There is no timer. It stays until you take action.

❏ File naming - Make consistent choices regarding naming your digital files. Remember that you will need to find these files fast when your boss or customer is demanding them to be messaged to you immediately. With all of the files in my Creative Cloud, I highly recommend an easy system to remember how to search for them again. Suggestions include by date, customer, project name, building name, city, or event. Remember, your coworkers will need to access these files as you share the workload and need to move various projects around to different departments. Also, they will need to access them when you are on sick leave or move on to your next job.

❏ Update your resumé, CV, or portfolio - Add your latest projects and awards to your portfolio and resumé. Does your Behance professional portfolio show your skills to their best advantage? It's best to fill it with work that you wish to do moving forward. Keeping old work will have your potential customers and employers assuming that is the type of work you prefer to do. Move old work to your archive pages.

❑ What other professional software do you use? I had downloaded an app used to place orders for delivery by my local printer, but sadly, they have since gone out of business. Delete this old software from your system that is taking up space.

PRO Tip: Visit the software company's forums and do a little bit of research on the programs you use. It's time to take a concerted effort to organize your work. Spending even half an hour of additional learning on the programs you already have can make a huge difference in your decision to either keep them or delete them. Direct questions you have about the software here. Ask the software's representative. Ask your in-house company communications team to see if others are having the same issue.

Which industry-specific software do you use? There are databases from simple systems to Customer Relationship Management (CRM) to gantt charts in use.

❑ Professional Organizations - e.g. Engineering, Farming, Restaurateur, etc.

❑ Professional social media accounts - Check LinkedIn, professional engineers' online sites, and other professional organizations' websites where you need to always keep an up-to-date professional image and credentials. This includes professional organizations' individual websites and other social media pages managed by your specific industry.

❑ Professional photo profile images - Do they need to be specific to your position? Have you received a promotion and you need a new profile to reflect the change from a previously outdoor position to your new indoor management position?

❑ Professional contact information - Do you have a professional email and other contact information? It is usually some form of your real name and set up in a way that you'll remember to access it. For creative and performance artists that sometimes use stage names, is your name and message consistently on-brand throughout the various points of contact?

❏ Update your promotions and awards - When you receive a new award, put it up on your profile right away. Same with promotions and new training certifications. Letting these actions sit and not adding them until you suddenly need to will only add a lot of stress at a time when you can least afford it. You'll be ready for the next opportunity when it comes knocking. Being able to immediately respond to serendipitous opportunities shows an organized person.

❏ Location-specific memberships - Some professional organizations are location specific. Have you moved? Should you transfer your membership to the new location?

❏ Professional click circuit - Create a separate professional click circuit, as discussed in Chapter 11, for each of the professional stops you need to make on the internet to ensure you connect with various clients, your bosses, your current and previous coworkers, and those that you supervise.

❏ Service levels - Which level of service do you need from your industry software? There are often different levels of monthly and annual fees to use various industry software. Are you comfortable with your level of service? Can you use a less feature-heavy level and save some money? Or will purchasing a more expensive tier of features level up your business?

You're the expert - Create a general checklist to be used for each of the operating system's professional software you use. Time to persevere! If you don't have a decluttering or maintenance system in place, now is the time to create one. Scheduling your maintenance organization in your calendar will block out the time you need for upkeep.

Decluttering maintenance check-in:
❏ Update your monthly stats - Be accountable for the results. Post

your wins, post your failures, and re-affirm your promise to yourself to complete the process. Tweak your habits to suit your changing schedule. New projects and new jobs create upheavals in any smooth schedule along with changes in family dynamics. Children returning to school or the start of summer break create a need for you to update the consistent habits you need to complete your digital decluttering.

29 - Travel: Business & Personal

Traveling within your own country for both business and personal reasons will result in more stay-cations in your future. It's time to support and enjoy what your own local areas have to offer. Personal vacation time should be just that, vacation time. Reduce your screen time, too! This is a time to simply maintain your current levels of emails and documents and not stress about pushing for a big reduction in the numbers.

It's vacation; you will take a lot of photographs and they're going to be great. Mark in your schedule which day and time after your vacation you'll take to organize these photographs. You'll put together a fun slide show for the family after your return.

❑ Schedule the time necessary to edit your photos from your vacation. Think about how long it will take, schedule that time, then schedule at least three times that much time for a much more realistic timeframe to finish. Or is that just me who underestimates how much time this will take?

❑ Curate your travel apps - Many of the travel apps we use to get away from our own area are ones we can still use for more local getaways:

- ❏ Booking or Airbnb for places to stay.
- ❏ Travelocity for information on the areas and reviews.
- ❏ Reviews - Leave a review of your experiences; these businesses have been hit hard recently and could use the help if you had a great experience visiting them. Give a tip or two for future visitors.

- ❏ Screenshots of various ticket QR codes - I always take a screenshot of my tickets and QR codes I need for entry. I would hate to arrive at the airport or a museum and find I no longer had a phone signal or internet connection and couldn't continue with my travels. Delete them after you no longer need them.

- ❏ Language dictionary - You are going to have several apps for the unique needs of your international life. Be sure each app you have has true value to you and isn't clutter around your most valuable apps. As I travel, I like to know how to say a few polite phrases in the local language. Plus, I live in Japan, far away from my home country, so I have at least three different language apps at my fingertips to ensure I have the best communication possible.

For business travels, you'll still likely need a lot of screen time, but if there are steps you can take to minimize any increases in your email numbers, do so.
- ❏ Set up your email's out-of-office settings.

- ❏ Set your voicemail messages regarding your business trip or holiday time, including another contact in the company who may be able to help them.

Scan your receipts and review them for your business claims.
- ❏ Airline tickets and miles
- ❏ Rental car receipts and programs
- ❏ Hotel receipts

Enjoy your vacation and plan for curating that new set of photographs and video you took while away. For business travelers, make time to file your receipts and reports for reimbursements.

30 - Food

Our entire food chain is electronically connected, from Community Supported Agriculture (CSA) boxes to grocery and restaurant delivery to our favorite pizza place. Each organization has their own app or at least their own pay portal.

❑ Grocery delivery apps - Grocery delivery has come a long way in the last couple of years with most grocers offering a delivery option within their own apps. Other stores and online retailers like Target and Amazon are in on grocery delivery, also. The system could use a lot of work, but by now you know who is most reliable in the game.
❑ Delete the most egregious deliverers.
❑ Edit your grocery list. You like that the app remembers what you have ordered, but sometimes you wish you hadn't ordered that one item or those weird chips. Ensure you don't order it again by removing it from your list.

❑ CSA Boxes - Periodically review your options with your CSA. With different growing seasons, they can change what you can have delivered, the pricing structures, frequency of deliveries, or even the locations of deliveries. Most provide announcements through their newsletters, but just in case you missed it or accidentally deleted it in your email culling, check their website for the most up-to-date information.

Have your CSA contact information set in your phone contacts to make updates to your deliveries. Make it easy to modify your deliveries in the case of vacations and business trips when you will be away from home.

❏ Meal deliveries - There are so many restaurants offering deliveries and take away that it's impossible to have an app for each. Consolidated delivery apps can be problematic, so make your delivery app choices carefully. Check the meal delivery options available to you and delete the ones that are no longer available, don't work, or you don't like anymore.

❏ Pizza delivery app - Probably the most popular ones are pizza delivery apps. Are you happy with the setup you have on your phone app?

❏ Cooking recipe websites and apps - I love my Japanese Cookpad app! Any time I am in the grocery store and see a new ingredient I'm unsure of how to use when cooking, I look it up on Cookpad to see how others have used it in recipes. I highly recommend this for adventurous cooks and foodies when living in a country much different than the one in which you learned to cook.

❏ Curate your recipe apps and websites - Keep the ones you love and delete the cooking recipe experiments that were not successful.

Take control of your food options to stay as healthy as possible using the most financially advantageous and convenient way possible. You'll probably need to make adjustments throughout the year depending upon the school, vacations, family obligations, and holidays. For example, when you go away on vacation, be sure to let your CSA delivery know you won't need a box that week.

31 - Education

When the days get shorter and the homework starts rolling in, it's best to be proactive when it comes to you and your family's education. Since that is not always possible, let's declutter what you have and then take steps to get ahead of this coming semester or the next school year.

Get ready with your password system as you know this involves multiple websites, each with their own password.
❏ Old homework projects and assignments - Choose which ones to keep and which ones to delete. If you are not ready to decide and you have enough data space available, you can shovel it all into a single archive folder marked by year, by class, by instructor, or by each child's name. As the archives age you'll have a better idea of which files are most important that you need to keep, and you'll delete the unnecessary files.
❏ Delete bookmarks to websites to activities you no longer participate in.
❏ File with payment information for your records.
❏ Folders with important information for additional schooling and resumé building such as SAT score records, Graduation information, etc.

Current education activities:

Keep your current homework in an easily accessible area—either in the cloud or on your device—and a place you feel comfortable to back up your current homework assignments—either in a second place in the cloud or on an external drive space such as a USB.
- Homework portals - Keep passwords stored in your comfortable password system as discussed in Chapter 12.
- After school activities - Don't forget that each of these activities can also have an impact on college entrance, so keep awards and other achievement records in an easy to find folder. From sports to music to videography and more, each activity probably also has its own need for passwords. Include these in your password system.
- Bookmark the websites for the current semesters activities.

Be Proactive!
While culling and organizing your piles of digital homework clutter, you probably started to see patterns of which classes had a lot of homework and which ones required a lot of storage space like a videography class, and now that another semester of classes are starting soon, you should put together your homework data system now.
- Choose where your files and folders will be stored for easy access and for easy saving when in a rush out the door. NOTE: Don't just save the folders on your desktop. Remember that too many and too large of files saved on your desktop will slow down your computer.
- Bookmark the websites for the current semesters activities.
- Keep an admin folder of your payments made, classes signed up for, classes dropped. Mistakes happen; save yourself the headache later and be ready to resolve any questions that may come up.
- Load the contact information of your instructors and your school admin or keep a file in the same folder with your other class homework so long as it's easily accessible.

Education is a lifelong achievement. You continue to be curious about various subjects long after you've graduated.

- Subscriptions to learning sites - Are you learning new skills from Lynda, Udemy, or a SkillShare subscription? If it's an annual subscription, be sure to mark your calendar before the year is up to either cancel before a new year is charged to your credit card or investigate if that learning portal is the best option for you. Did you forget you even had a subscription to it, incurring monthly charges for nothing? Or are you regularly using just one service and not others at this time? You can only learn so much at a time, so be judicious in your choices or you will just be throwing your money away. Cancel the others. There will always be the option to sign up again, even to capture another sale price to make it happen!

❑ Webinars - How many webinars have you participated in? Do you still have the class information cluttering about in your files? Some of it is excellent information, yet other pieces are no longer necessary to keep. Delete the ones you no longer need.

Choose a filing system for the previous classes you want to keep. Make it easy to add new class information as you continue your lifelong learning. Are you currently taking any webinars or online classes?

❑ Online meeting apps - Are your meeting apps such as Zoom or Skype on the right devices? Delete and add the apps as necessary, being sure to update the software along the way.

❑ Are your headphones and microphone ready for the next online class? Learn how your new wireless earbuds work before your next session.

❑ Monthly or 100-day projects - A good habit ritual can remind you to play each day, experiment with your materials, and then post your results on your preferred social media account. Do you have files ready to place those photos in? Are your digital mediums like Adobe Fresco or Procreate apps up to date? Are your brushes ready? With prompts handy, I download the prompt image and keep it in the same file as my completed sketches.

Declutter your digital classroom(as an instructor):
❑ Class assignments - This is a lot of storage, as it isn't usually just one class or two, it is multiple classes, multiple interviews, and multiple conversations with students and other experts that will

be available to your students for at least a year or more depending upon your program. Video can be stored on sites such as Vimeo or WordPress sites with a student password.

❑ Meeting software - How will you conduct the meeting? Via Zoom, Skype, etc.?

❑ Website - Are there clear explanations as to what each student will learn and how their life will change for the better by taking the course.

❑ Homework assignments - How will you give and receive homework with your students? Will you provide a Google document or Dropbox account or will you email information back and forth?

❑ Payment - How will students pay you? Is your payment system up to date? (PayPal, Square, Apple Pay, etc.) It's best to have multiple ways to receive funds in case there is a glitch in one system or a student needs to use another option.

Each of these options should be checked for cluttered works, keeping things neat, and easy accessibility, which will continue to leave a good impression on the students as they become experts in the subject you're teaching.

32 - Auto

Make your commute productive . . . or at least entertaining. I saw in a documentary years ago that Japanese people spend approximately seven years of their life commuting on trains. No idea if it's true, but it got me thinking about what you could do with seven years of your time in your car, on the train, or on the bus to and from work.

As you travel on your commute, think about all the ways to make it a better environment during your next commute. Last time I rented a car, it had all the bells and whistles. It had a tablet-like command center for all the controls, USB charging ports, and hands-free phone features, and it was as distracting as a disco dance club while I was driving down the street.

Take action to digitally declutter your car and get it set up just right for your daily commute. Your options will depend upon your vehicle; choose what will make your commute better.
❏ Hands-free smartphone setup - Is your smartphone correctly connected? If it's been giving you trouble, now's the time to fix it.

❏ Audiobooks
❏ Podcasts
❏ Movies for your children and other passengers

Radio settings:
- ❏ Set your radio to the best stations - Is your favorite music ready to go? Do you want to make your trip fruitful with podcasts or do you need the entertainment of a comedian to wind down from a stressful day?
- ❏ Be sure to keep the one station with the best, up-to-date traffic reports.
- ❏ Is the clock set to the correct time?
- ❏ Temperature settings
- ❏ Nav-System
- ❏ Automatic pay toll system - Is the toll system for your area set up correctly?
- ❏ Dashboard video camera set up

This may create a quarterly goal of an optimal commute to learn a foreign language or about local flora and fauna via a podcast, or provide entertainment for your child. Imagine it as a less stressful mode of transportation for everyone.

- ❏ Set up your commute for getting work done. Is your smartphone set up for taking dictation? Create messages for coworkers and verbal reminders to yourself. Are you ready to dictate your novel that you would like to complete during your long commute?

Time to make these ideas happen. Time to make your commute tolerable, entertaining, or even productive. Think about where you'd like to be in three months or a year.

I found additional transportation apps on my phone that I used over the years.
- ❏ Lyft and Uber apps
- ❏ Scooter app from a trip to Paris
- ❏ Bicycle apps from Hawai'i

I will use a couple of these transportation apps in the future, but I'm definitely not using the scooters again.

33 - Periodic Decluttering Maintenance

PRO Tip: Write these maintenance check-ins into your calendar right away, before your schedule becomes overrun. You'll know to schedule other appointments around your periodic decluttering maintenance. Be patient with yourself; over time, your periodic maintenance will be less and less burdensome as general practices around your digital assets will be more and more organized. Your daily habits and organization will become much more smooth and automatic.

❑ Long-term and short-term goals - What did you set as your long-term and short-term goals as recommended in Chapter 4? Did you mark what your long-term, monthly, or yearly goal was from the start of your decluttering process? Did you set reasonable goals and have been meeting them along the way? Did you make adjustments along the way to accommodate life's various upheavals yet are still making progress? Complete the small daily and weekly actions and the long-term goal will be accomplished. Keep your end goal in mind as you mark your progress in your stats. Reference the examples in Appendix I and II.

❑ Go through all of the decluttering in waves. Scrape away at layers and years of data accumulation. Unsure whether or not to save or delete a photo? That's okay. You'll make a solid decision in the next wave.

☐ Accountability partners - Bring your friends along for the challenge and the check-ins to keep focused on your decluttering quest.

Daily Maintenance
AM Launch:
☐ Check new emails and messages:
Answer those that are vital, such as family emergencies. Delete those that are garbage.
Answer the rest during your regularly scheduled email time.
☐ Click Circuit

Evening Setup:
☐ Clear out the remainder of the day's emails
☐ Backup your work
☐ Clear off your desktop

Weekly:
☐ Empty downloads folder
☐ Empty trash
☐ Close or bookmark browser tabs
☐ Check for website updates

Monthly:
☐ Accountability - Check-in with your friends, accountability group, and admin group. At a minimum, these check-ins are done monthly. Weekly check-ins can be even better, and depending upon schedules and friendships, it can even be daily. Definitely do monthly check-ins even after you've completed the initial digital decluttering. It'll be an important stopgap in keeping your digital life from growing out of control again.
☐ Progress check - Not done? Be thankful for your progress to this point, as every little bit helps.
☐ Back up your website
☐ Install updates, including:
    ☐ Plug-ins
    ☐ Extensions
☐ Unsubscribe from newsletters

❑ Mark your progress - You can do so visually with things such as gumballs or marbles in a jar. You can also keep track in a line graph after entering the numbers into a spreadsheet.

Take a look at where you are now in your decluttering and notice how much progress you have made so far. You have tackled a large piece of the big picture each month. It takes a lot of persistent hard work to slow the clutter monster, but you can do this. You have a good idea of what needs to happen next to see this big project through. When you get stuck in the weeds, reread Chapter 11 where I give you tips and encouragement regarding long-term projects. By the end of another month or a year, you'll look back and see that by taking the next step, moving forward into the tasks, and continuing to declutter, your digital life will be a huge weight lifted.

Quarterly or 90-day check-in:
❑ Check your notifications - Adjust as necessary
❑ Curate your social media - unfollow or delete
❑ Review your browser's bookmarks and favorites

The 90-day check-in is in keeping with the quarterly flow of business already in place. It is also considered a long enough time to show progress on a long-term project yet short enough for you to breathe, maintain your energy level, and make small updates. This doesn't negate your need for the monthly check-ins or the weekly admin check-ins or posting your stats at least twice each week. Each check-in is keeping your promise to yourselves. Each check-in is reminding us to keep your eyes on the bright, shiny goal. Don't get distracted by details and actions that aren't important to reaching your goal.

When each quarter ends, it's a good idea to see exactly how much work you have accomplished decluttering. Type in your updated spreadsheet numbers, post your habit tracker tics, and celebrate your progress. Realize you are slowing down the floodwaters to a trickle, or maybe you have been able to make a massive dent and completely reverse the flow in the first quarter. A quarterly check-in brings us back to our big goal of a clean and clear decluttered digital life.

Regularly scheduling your progress check-ins will reap rewards for your long-term declutter maintenance. Marking your progress and seeing your stats move will be such a relief. The small regular reminders and the time already blocked out for the task in the future will help ensure you maintain the progress you have worked so hard to achieve.

34 - Congratulations, You've Taken Command of Your Digital Life!

You started this journey with a huge pile of digital clutter. You've re-homed the stray digital dust bunnies and swept out the electronic cobwebs.

You resolved to complete your decluttering task, and your end goal has been achieved!

You are likely feeling relieved, more relaxed, and empowered as you now own your work versus your digital assets overwhelming you. Over the past weeks, months, or even years, you have slowly and progressively reduced your digital clutter, created good organizing habits, and found that simply turning on your computer is a much more relaxing experience. Rather than the power button being an "on" button for your stress, eye strain, headaches, and the sense of overwhelming dread, you will have taken your digital life down to size, because you are now in control.

You are ready to calmly start each day on a positive note when you hit the power button, because you now have the power. This newly organized, decluttered digital life is a welcome relief. You are easily able to track down each file you need.

You have made good choices regarding where you spend your money on digital services. You have right-sized your data storage. How much money are you now saving by right-sizing your digital life? By organizing your files, you were able to see where you had extra storage space and where you needed more. By adjusting your data storage and asset allocations, you are now organized in such a way as to maximize your time and money.

You are prepared for emergencies. Whether you experience a typhoon, fire, flood, or loss of your device, you are ready for when an emergency happens. You're ready to bug-out when the typhoon hits, or the fires come, or the flooding makes its way to your home. You are more flexible and will be ready to pivot when your life takes a tight curve in the road, such as needing to quickly move locations for a job or family needs. You are ready when that sudden job transfer includes transferring the children's school info and moving all of your possessions.

You are ready to enjoy a successful digital detox experience; remember that taking a break is a break, not simply an ostrich-style escape.

You've taken command of your digital life. You are ready when the boss demands to see that proposal rough draft immediately! You know exactly which files contain the pieces of the proposal as your team has understood the organizing system. You're able to compile the latest drafts into a single file and forward it to the boss or simply direct the boss to the correct file.

For those of us who are already leading a minimalist life, it is great to do the same with our digital life—keeping it minimal and streamlining its efficiency so we can keep our data storage for only the most essential items.

Periodically go through your digital files in waves. Oftentimes, your digital clutter will be seen with fresher eyes and circumstances in the second or third waves of decluttering. The first or second time you will likely still have files you are unsure about keeping or deleting. You'll find you can let go of them in the next wave, or the next—or new technology will be created for you to let go of it.

Remember, this is not a once through and done project. More digital assets will continue to accumulate, others will become obsolete, and storage options will change. Scheduling regular intervals to declutter your digital assets will keep all of this hard work you've just accomplished together. That's why it's necessary to schedule regular maintenance.

Maintenance of your digital files will continue to get easier as you quickly recognize your options with each piece of digital asset you receive. After going through all of your digital assets, you'll have come across quite a few that you weren't sure about deleting yet. With all you have learned, you will realize immediately when there is a problem and have a good idea of what you need to do to declutter it.

Congratulations! You are a digital minimalist.

Appendix I
Digital Life List - Spreadsheet Example

	A	B	C	D	E	F	G	H	I
1			Data Provided	Data Avail	Week 1	Week 2	Week 3		...Week 16
2									
3	**Emails - Personal**								
4	Email #1		15GB		1503	1497	1216		4
5	Email #2		15GB		2802	2202	2000		4
6	Email #3		5GB		117	0	0		0
7									
8	Photographs		50GB		4390	3997	3901		1709
9	Videos		inluded in above		131	52	49		11
10									
11	**Emails - Business**								
12	Email #1		50GB		317	325	231		2
13	Email #2		50GB		14	0	0		0
14	Accounting Software		XGB						
15									
16	**External Devices**								
17	SDD 5TB		5TB	1.2GB	1.2	1.2	0.7		0.5
18	USB - Blue		16GB	8.4GB	8.4	8.4	8.4		1.2
19	USB Black		16GB	16GB	16	16	2.2		2.2
20	SDcard #1		256MB	35MB	35	35	35		35
21									
22	**Cloud**								
23	iCloud		50GB	3.3GB	3.3GB	4.6 v			
24	*additional purchase		200GBTTL	127GB			145.2		103
25	Adobe Creative Cloud		100GB	74GB	74GB	72	68		62
26									
27	**Devices**								
28	Laptop 2012		750GB						
29	Laptop 2020		500GB	394GB	397	381	227		225.2
30	Tablet		128GB	73.5GB	74.2	66.8	54		61.2
31	Smartphone		64GB	26GB	27	35.3	30		21

Appendix II
Digital Life List: Mind mapping

Thank You!

I very much appreciate you taking the time to read *Digital Declutter: The BIG Checklist to obtain digital minimalism*. I hope you found *The BIG Checklist* useful and are following the tips and check ins along the way to a digitally decluttered life. I and potential readers would appreciate it if you left a review, thank you!

Find more information by visiting
https://www.digitaldeclutterCEO.com

Follow on Twitter for more tips:
@declutterceo

Acknowledgments

Thank you goes to all the other authors who failed to write a checklist as large as my digital clutter. Their inadequate lists prompted me to create my own checklist to share.

Ever so grateful to my creative friends who listened, advised, and supported: Lori, Eva, Robin, Chloe, Misheru, Louise, and Janette. Special thanks go to my new writing friends; Linda, Anna, Marissa, Lily, Eucharia, and Joan.

Thank you to The Bearded Editor, for the help ensuring *The BIG Checklist* is coherent for others to read.

Thank you also belongs to The Design Trust and 20Books to 50K for an innumerable amount of information to help make this book a success!

Special thank you to my husband for all the support and adventures, looking forward to many more!

Notes

Introduction
KonMari Philosophy Archives – KonMari: The Official Website of Marie Kondo. (n.d.). Retrieved September 10, 2020, from https://konmari.com/category/konmari-philosophy/

Ch 1 Your Current Digital Mess
North, M., Sparrowhawk, & Pedro. (2019, November 28). Abstaining From Social Media Doesn't Improve Well-Being, Experimental Study Finds. Retrieved Nov 29, 2019, from https://digest.bps.org.uk/2019/11/28/abstaining-from-social-media-doesnt-improve-well-being-experimental-study-finds/

Ch 3 Charting Your Digital Life
TEDx Talks. (n.d.). Want to learn better? Start mind mapping | Hazel Wagner | TEDxNaperville https://youtu.be/5nTuScU70As

Ch 6 Three BIG Steps to Jump-start Your Decluttering
How Lack of Sleep Impacts Cognitive Performance and Focus. (2020, June 02). Retrieved July 17, 2020, from https://www.sleepfoundation.org/articles/how-lack-sleep-impacts-cognitive-performance-and-focus

What is ASMR? (2020, January 23). Retrieved July 23, 2020, from https://www.sleep.org/articles/what-is-asmr/

Ch 10 Emails & Good Habits
Espeon, N. (2016). Manage your e-mails with the "Inbox Zero" method. Retrieved June 22, 2020, from https://www.nicoespeon.com/en/2016/02/manage-emails-inbox-zero/

Ch 11 Habits for the Long Term
Rubin, G. Stop Expecting to Change Your Habit in 21 Days. (2009, October 21). Retrieved June 22, 2020, from https://www.psychologytoday.com/us/blog/the-happiness-project/200910/stop-expecting-change-your-habit-in-21-days

Clear, J. (2019, January 21). The Ultimate Habit Tracker Guide: Why and How to Track Your Habits. Retrieved June 22, 2020, from https://jamesclear.com/habit-tracker

Ch 13 Emergency!
.gov, F. (2014). Digital Disaster Prep: Are You Ready? Retrieved June 17, 2020, from https://www.fema.gov/news-release/2014/09/05/digital-disaster-prep-are-you-ready

Ch 15 Home, Pets, & the Internet of Things
Burgess, M. (2018, February 16). What is the Internet of Things? WIRED explains. Retrieved July 22, 2020, from https://www.wired.co.uk/article/internet-of-things-what-is-explained-iot

Ch 26 Reading
McCarthy, J. (2020, June 01). In U.S., Library Visits Outpaced Trips to Movies in 2019. Retrieved July 17, 2020, from https://news.gallup.com/poll/284009/library-visits-outpaced-trips-movies-2019.aspx

About the Author

D.M. Elliot is a curry-loving creative who passive-aggressively ignored her hordes of digital dust bunnies for years.

A determined, self-proclaimed minimalist, Elliot searched for a solution to organize her digital clutter and discovered checklists as the solution. Through her decluttering journey of combining checklists with good digital habits, she found a simple, step-by-step solution to right-size her digital life.

Creating The BIG Checklist allowed Elliot to organize and maintain a calm, digitally uncluttered, minimalist lifestyle. She lives with her husband in Japan.

www.ingramcontent.com/pod-product-compliance
Lightning Source LLC
Chambersburg PA
CBHW071452080526
44587CB00014B/2079